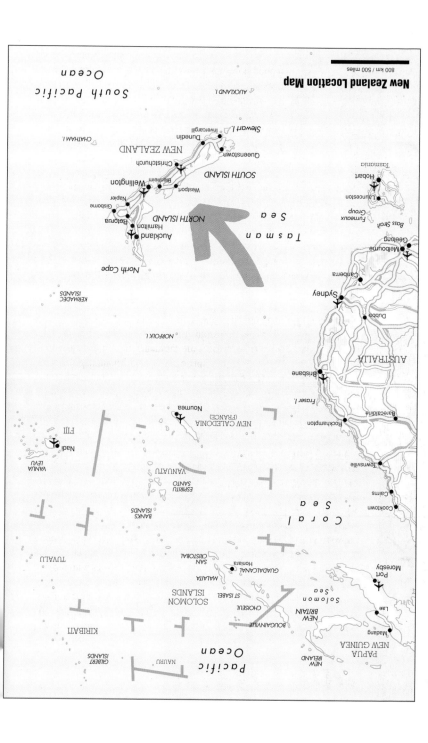

New Zealand Location Map

800 km / 500 miles

Welcome

This is one of 133 itinerary-based Pocket Guides produced by the editors of Insight Guides, whose books have set the standard for visual travel guides since 1970. With top-quality photography and authoritative recommendations, this guidebook brings you the very best of New Zealand in a series of tailor-made itineraries devised by Insight's correspondent and long-time New Zealand resident, Craig Dowling.

New Zealand is a unique country in many ways – its geography is both dramatic and expansive, and its population a diverse and welcoming mix of European, Maori, Polynesian and more recently Asian cultures. From the sub-tropical north to the temperate south, all the wonders of New Zealand are presented in the 18 itineraries contained in this guide. Using the five geographic hubs of Auckland, Rotorua and Wellington in the North Island, and Christchurch and Queenstown in the South Island as bases, the author covers a spectrum of dazzling sights: golden sand beaches washed by sparkling seas, grand fiords fringed by mighty rainforests, white glaciers carved through rugged mountains, swathes of fertile farmland grazed by sheep, and both cosmopolitan cities and quaint small towns. The itineraries in this guide cover walking tours of the main city sights as well as day- and multi-day driving trips of the surrounding areas.

Complementing the itineraries are chapters on shopping, eating out and nightlife, and a fact-packed practical information section covering important travel essentials – including a run-down of the various outdoor activities which New Zealand is so famous for.

Craig Dowling was born in New Zealand. He lived for some years overseas, then returned to his homeland, recognising the balance of attractions that make New Zealand a wonderful place to live in and, with his wife Haidee, to bring up a young family. From having lived and worked first as a journalist and later in public relations roles in the country's three largest cities – Auckland, Wellington and Christchurch – Dowling has gained a broad insight into the diversity that makes New Zealand such a special place.

'It is a country in which you can savour simple pleasures mixed with a dash of adventure,' he says. 'From strolling along a beach and gazing at nearby islands, luxuriating in a thermal spring, and enjoying quality new-world wine, to swimming in a river fed by mountain rain and heading up that same mountain for views that seem to stretch forever…. If you enjoy a vacation that is good for the soul, New Zealand is the place to visit.'

6   contents

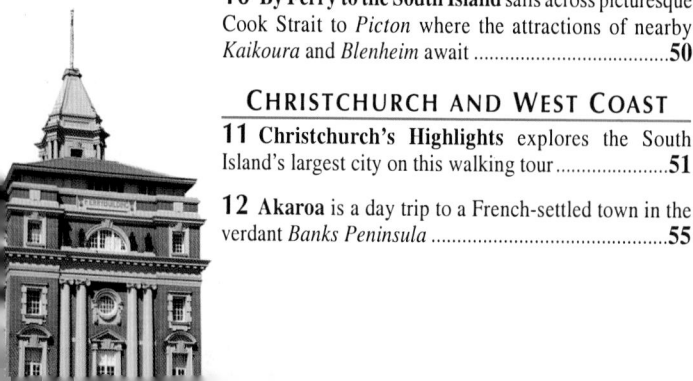

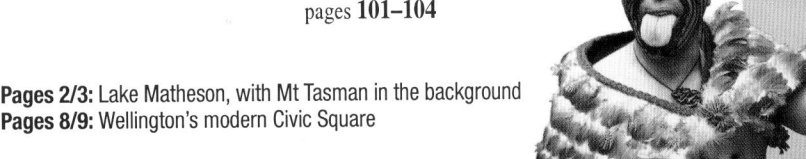

Pages 2/3: Lake Matheson, with Mt Tasman in the background
Pages 8/9: Wellington's modern Civic Square

history/culture

History & Culture

New Zealand, by European standards, is a young country. No one should travel there expecting to find the trappings of history and culture that manifest themselves in the monuments, museums and castles familiar to Europe. This is not to say there is no distinguishable 'Kiwi culture', just that it is a culture that is still evolving and seeking to define itself. Elements of it are reflected in the concept of 'mateship' – an understated loyalty to friends, and a sense of humour that often borders on the laconic. New Zealanders also have a reputation for innovation, which is borne out of the country's geographic isolation. A fresh approach to life and living is reflected in the art, music and cuisine of the country. Like its nearest neighbour Australia, New Zealand positions itself among the 'New World' countries.

At the same time, New Zealand is a Pacific nation and its indigenous culture is Polynesian Maori. It was only relatively recently, in historical terms, that the country was settled by Europeans. These settlers came mainly from England, Scotland and Ireland, and their influence dominated the country through much of the 20th century. Recently, however, a more multi-cultural society has developed – while English and Maori are the official languages, you may also hear Samoan, Tongan and several Asian languages spoken.

Making its Mark

In a country where sports is accorded the status of a minor religion (rugby is the country's national game), recognition has been hard won by artists like Charles F Goldie (1870–1947) and Colin McCahon (1919–1987). Nevertheless, New Zealand's coterie of artists and writers continue to make an impact on the world stage. Drawing on a mixture of colonial and indigenous influences, writers like Janet Frame (1924–2004) and Booker Prize winner Keri Hume follow in the tradition of one of the country's greatest literary exports, Katherine Mansfield (1888–1923). New Zealand has its music and its musicians too, ranging from symphony orchestras to the likes of pop star Neil Finn and his former band Crowded House. And let's not forget New Zealander Peter Jackson, director of the acclaimed *Lord of the Rings* trilogy, actors like Russell Crowe and Sam Neill, nor acclaimed comedy playwright Roger Hall, when assessing the country's growing sense of national identity.

In terms of social movements, New Zealand has been influenced by forces from Western Europe (especially the UK) and the US, adopting ideas and turning them into action with often more vigour than the countries from where the ideas originated. In the late 19th century for instance, New Zealand became the first country to grant universal suffrage to women. Amidst the economic pressures of the first half of the 20th century, New Zealand

Left: Arthur's Pass (South Island) in spring
Right: Maori in full battle regalia

developed one of the most advanced systems of social welfare for its people.

These and other efforts serve to illustrate a common feature of New Zealanders. If a job has to be done, there will be someone prepared to do it. This, and an easy going attitude – encapsulated in the common Kiwi phrase 'she'll be right' – partly explain the number of New Zealanders who have distinguished themselves on the world stage. These are people like Sir Ernest Rutherford (1876–1937), the Nobel prize-winning scientist; Sir Edmund Hillary (1919–), who in 1953 made the first successful ascent of Mount Everest; and Dame Kiri Te Kanawa (1944–), the renowned opera diva.

New Zealand is looking both to the future and back to its past as it forges a national identity unique to its Pacific shores. Maori language and culture are increasingly taught in schools, and important aspects of that culture – its affinity with the natural world, and its respect for the family unit, for instance – are now drawn upon and valued by the wider non-Maori community. These cultural themes are commonly explored in traditional Maori arts and crafts. Travellers to New Zealand should look out for the works of a new generation of carvers, sculptors and craftspeople who are using their traditional skills to confront modern issues such as alienation and social tension, with often remarkable and challenging results.

The Lonely Islands

The level of achievement is quite startling, given the fact that the country's population is just over 4 million. And it is even more startling when you look at the relatively short time span that New Zealand has existed as a nation. For the greater part of its existence, New Zealand was uninhabited by land mammals, aside from two species of bat. For some 100 million years, up until perhaps only the last 1,000 years, New Zealand developed in isolation from everywhere and everything, save the forces of nature.

The land was forested by large native conifers such as the kauri. Ancient animals which inhabited the undergrowth included reptiles like the tuatara, large ground snails, and, in the absence of predators, several native bird species – the two most famous examples being the small kiwi and the huge

but now extinct moa – who, lacking the need, lost their ability to fly. They were joined on the ground by flightless insects like the large weta.

Seeds, travelling on winds and wings to the islands, brought a diversity to the flora that is a distinct feature of New Zealand to this day.

First Footsteps

And then came the human factor – but not for thousands of years. Indications are that a gradual migration into the Western Pacific some 4,000 years ago led first to the development of the distinctive Polynesian culture, and ultimately to the first human footprints being made in about the 10th century, on the islands which were called Aotearoa.

Left: a tattooed Maori *rangatira* (chief)

By the 12th century, settlements were scattered over most of the country. And having had few or no continuing contacts with the outside world, these settlements developed unique characteristics which are now recognised as Maori culture.

The Maori people developed a communal society based on groups of varying sizes, ranging from the extended family grouping, or *whanau* (pronounced 'far-now'), to large tribes, or *iwi* (pronounced 'ee-we'). Tribes were organised around a *rangatira* (chief) while family groupings were headed by the *kaumatua* (group of elders). Maori livelihood was ensured by the subsistence farming of root crops such as the delicious *kumara*, a type of sweet potato, and supplemented by activities such as fishing, hunting and food gathering.

Inter-tribal warfare was a common feature of early Maori life, though not on a huge scale. However, when the growing population put pressure on the asset most prized by the Maori – their land – a system of fortified villages, or *pa*, was developed. Although often warlike, there was a lot more to the early Maori. The *pa*, for example, often featured buildings with elaborately carved facades; and art, music, dance and an oral literary tradition reached a high level of refinement.

Maori tradition combines a strong awareness of an individual's social responsibilities along with a fierce spiritual affinity to the natural environment, the source of fascinating myths and legends. Their culture at this time, however, neither held any particular world view nor entertained concepts of nationhood or race. As the Maori began to encounter Europeans, they saw the latter only as members of another, albeit strange, rival tribe and probably had little idea as to the profound influence they would exert on the future of the islands of Aotearoa.

More Company

The first recorded visit to the land of Aotearoa by Europeans came in December 1642 when Dutch explorer Abel Tasman sighted the west coast of the South Island from his ship. Abel Tasman proved himself not very able by initially naming the sighting as Staten Landt, mistaking it for part of South America. He mapped a small stretch of the coast, but was attacked by Maori tribesmen while anchoring near what is now known as Golden Bay (he called it 'Murderers'

Above: a Maori *pa* (fortified village)
Right: indigenous art

Bay'). Tasman left without setting foot on the land.

That inauspicious beginning may have been partly to blame for the hiatus in European exploration of the region, for it was not until 1769 that British explorer Captain James Cook advanced new knowledge of New Zealand. Captain Cook circumnavigated the entire country, and his charts and journals made the land known to the outside world. Indeed, he took a fancy to the land himself, returning there for two more visits, in 1773–74 and 1777.

In the late 1700s and early 1800s, New Zealand developed as an offshoot of New South Wales in Australia. The Anglican chaplain to the New South Wales Penal Colony, Rev Samuel Marsden, set up the first mission station in New Zealand in 1814; about the same time when whalers made landings and set up stations of their own type on the New Zealand coast.

Colonisation

Progressively, other settlements were established on its land, and European crops and cropping methods were introduced to the Maori people. Their reactions were varied, to say the least. Some Maori were happy to comply in order to obtain the strange gifts (often blankets and muskets) of the *Pakeha* (white settlers). Others were openly antagonistic. And still many more were ambivalent. In fact, when British sovereignty was proclaimed over New Zealand in 1840, there were many inland Maori who had still never met a *Pakeha*.

The pace of white settlement quickened after sovereignty was declared, with a rush for land led by the New Zealand Company. In 1852, a General Assembly was established by the British Constitution Act. However, the protection supposedly offered to the Maori in the 1840 signing of the Treaty of Waitangi *(see pages 30–31)* failed to materialise.

Land was bought for often ridiculously low prices, traditional Maori values were undermined and *Pakeha* diseases proved virulent to a native population who had little or no developed immunity. This led to a series of clashes known as the New Zealand Wars in the 1860s. The outcome was inconclusive and resulted in the further dispiriting of the Maori population and the increased momentum in the process of colonisation.

The discovery of gold in the rivers of the central South Island led to an economic boom for the European settlers while the subsequent development of technology to ship frozen meat to Britain further established a platform for New Zealand's growth and development as a provider of agricultural products to Europe.

Wide-ranging social reforms took place in the 1880s, and in 1893, New Zealand became the first country in the world

Above: the mountain named after Cook
Left: New Zealand state flag

where women could vote in the national elections. A system of old age welfare pensions was also introduced, giving New Zealand a reputation as 'the social laboratory of the world', as one prominent writer at the time described it.

The Twentieth Century

New Zealand moved from the status of a colony to a Dominion (a self-governing territory) of the British Empire in 1907, but strong loyalist links saw tens of thousands of New Zealand soldiers serve the Allied cause in World War I. New Zealand soldiers distinguished themselves but in no place more than during the ill-fated campaign in Gallipoli, Turkey. ANZAC Day on 25 April, commemorating the lives lost in that battle, is now a public holiday in New Zealand, and Gallipoli is seen as an important event in the development of the nation's patriotic identity.

New Zealand suffered with everyone else in the depression of the 1930s. Bloody riots took place and disenchantment led to the election of the first Labour Government in 1935. By 1936, New Zealand's non-Maori population had grown to almost 1½ million, with distinct migration both northwards and into the cities. The Maori population had stabilised after being severely hit during an influenza pandemic in 1918 and hovered around the 60,000 mark. Land grievances were still a burning issue but the forum for debate had shifted into parliament. Influential Maori politicians who fought for the Maori cause include Sir Peter Buck, Hone Heke and Sir Apirana Ngata.

World War II again saw Kiwi soldiers fighting alongside the Allies. But significant changes were set in motion at this time. Firstly, the war stimulated a redirection of the country's trade to non-British markets. Secondly, post-war immigration from war-ravaged Europe coupled with a 'baby-boom' considerably boosted the country's population numbers.

New Developments

The post-war period can be divided into two distinct phases. An initial one of prosperity and near full employment, followed by a period of forced reappraisal of the country's position in the world. The event which shook New Zealand most was the entry of Britain into the European Economic Community in 1973 and its undertaking to buy meat and dairy products from other EEC members. New Zealand was suddenly faced with the disappearance of the major export market for its major export – agricultural products.

The trauma that this caused New Zealand was very real. But it also provided the impetus for New Zealand to forge ahead.

Right: agriculture is one of the pillars of New Zealand's economy

New Zealand Today

The country today is considerably more economically diverse than it was 40 years ago. The infrastructure is more balanced between primary, tertiary and secondary industries and there is an awareness of New Zealand being a Pacific country with a Pacific culture.

Close economic ties have been established with Australia, and, politically, New Zealand is becoming much more involved in world affairs on its own terms. New Zealanders have taken a strong moral stand on nuclear and

environmental issues and this has occasionally led to areas of diplomatic conflict with powers such as the US and France. The ANZUS Treaty between New Zealand, Australia and the US was effectively 'put on hold' after New Zealand refused a visit by an American nuclear-powered war-ship. And a Greenpeace vessel, the *Rainbow Warrior*, which was on its way to protest against French nuclear testing on a Pacific atoll, was bombed by French agents in Kiwi waters in 1985.

Internally, life was not always harmonious either. During the 1981 tour to New Zealand by the South African rugby team, thousands of anti-apartheid protesters clashed violently with police and rugby supporters. This and other events have made New Zealand a lot less naive than perhaps it once was.

There is a realisation that New Zealand is no longer isolated from world events, and that it can actually play a part in influencing the outcome of international issues. In recent years, it has lobbied for, and won a seat on the United Nations Security Council. Former New Zealand Prime Minister Mike Moore served a term as Director-General of the World Trade Organisation and in 1999, New Zealand hosted the APEC leaders' summit.

While young New Zealanders are still being tempted offshore in a tradition that has become known as 'the big OE' (overseas experience), this is being balanced by changes to immigration laws that are attracting a new group of skilled migrants to the country. Visitors will notice a strong Asian presence in some cities, and the flourishing of new cultures and cuisines.

If you are one of those attracted to New Zealand you will find that some things, thankfully, have not changed. Firstly, there is the inherent natural beauty of the country. And secondly, there is the charm of the people. Innocence may be on the way out, but it is not lost, and is still more easily found in New Zealand than in most other places in the world.

Above: Viaduct Basin awash with boats and cafés

HISTORY HIGHLIGHTS

1000 First Polynesian settlers.

1642 Discovery by Abel Tasman.

1769 Capt James Cook's first exploration of New Zealand.

1814 Rev Samuel Marsden establishes Anglican mission station.

1826 Attempt at European settlement under Capt Herd.

1840 Arrival of New Zealand Company's settlers. New Zealand annexed by New South Wales. Treaty of Waitangi is signed.

1841 New Zealand proclaimed independent of New South Wales.

1845 'Northern War' between Maori and *Pakeha*.

1852 Constitution Act passed. New Zealand divided into six provinces.

1854 First session of the General Assembly in Auckland.

1860 'Taranaki War' between *pakeha* and Maori.

1861 Gold discovery in Otago. First electric telegraph line opens.

1863 First steam railway opens.

1865 Seat of Government transferred to Wellington.

1870 New Zealand's first rugby match. Last battles of 'New Zealand Wars'.

1876 Provincial governments abolished.

1882 First shipment of frozen meat from New Zealand.

1886 Tarawera volcanic eruption.

1893 Universal female suffrage is introduced.

1907 Country granted Dominion status.

1908 North Island main trunk railway opens. Ernest Rutherford awarded Nobel Prize for Chemistry.

1914–18 World War I. Gallipoli campaign by ANZAC troops.

1918 Influenza epidemic.

1931 Hawkes Bay earthquake.

1935 First New Government elected.

1939–45 World War II. New Zealand Division serves in Italy.

1947 Statute of Westminster adopted by parliament.

1949 National Government elected.

1951 Prolonged waterfront industrial dispute. New Zealand signs ANZUS Treaty alliance with US and Australia.

1953 Sir Edmund Hillary successfully summits Mount Everest.

1965 Troops sent to Vietnam.

1967 Decimal system introduced.

1972 Labour Government elected.

1974 Christchurch hosts the Commonwealth Games.

1975 Waitangi Tribunal established to hear Maori land rights issues. National Government elected.

1981 Tour of New Zealand by South African rugby team leads to riots.

1983 Closer Economic Relations Agreement (CER) with Australia.

1984 Labour Government elected on anti-nuclear platform.

1985 Greenpeace protest vessel *Rainbow Warrior* bombed by French agents in New Zealand.

1986 Goods and Services Tax (GST) is introduced.

1990 Auckland hosts the Commonwealth Games. National Party wins general election.

1993 Electoral system changed to a proportional system called MMP.

1994 New Zealand wins America's Cup yachting regatta in San Diego.

1995 Waikato's Tanui tribe settles longstanding grievance claim.

1996 First MMP election. National Party forms coalition government with a minor party, New Zealand First.

1999 New Zealand hosts APEC summit and America's Cup yachting regatta. Labour Party coalition wins elections with Helen Clark as Prime Minister.

2002 Labour Party's Helen Clark is returned for second term as PM.

2003 Team New Zealand loses the America's Cup in Auckland. The population in New Zealand reaches 4 million. The final installment of Peter Jackson's *The Lord of the Rings* has its world premiere in Wellington.

2004 *The Lord of the Rings: The Return of the King* wins all of the 11 Academy Awards it was nominated for.

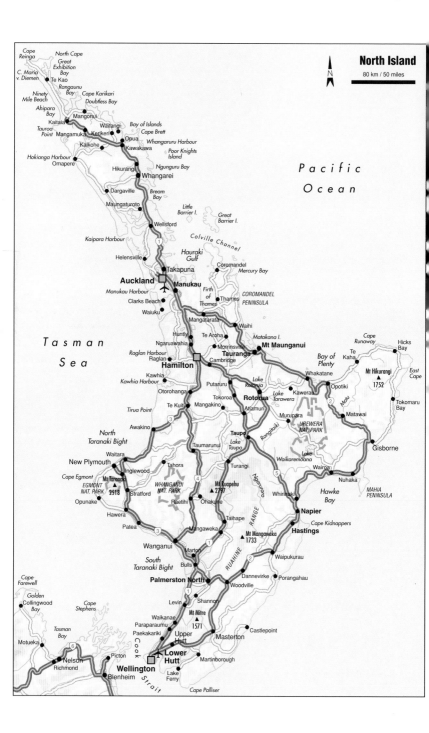

South Island

80 km / 50 miles

NORTH ISLAND

Wellington

SOUTH ISLAND

Tasman
Sea

Cape
Farewell
Farewell
Spit
Golden
Bay
Collingwood
D'Urville
Island
Cook Strait
Picton
Tasman
Bay
Blenheim
Motueka
Nelson
Richmond
Ward
TASMAN MTS
Karamea
Matupika
Karamea
Bight
Kawatiri
Junction
Owen
River
St Arnaud
Kaikoura
Westport
Mt Travers
2338
NELSON
LAKES
NAT. PARK
Hanmer
Springs
PAPAROA
NATIONAL PARK
Reefton
Springs
Junction
Waiau
Barrytown
Runanga
Greymouth
Ngahere
Culverden
Cheviot
Kumara Junction
Mt Longfellow
1898
Waipara
Hokitika
Otira
ARTHURS
PASS
NAT. PARK
Rangiora
Pegasus
Bay
Kaiapoi
Ross
Mt Murchison
2400
Oxford
Christchurch
Mt Whitcombe
2644
Springfield
Little
River
BANKS
PENINSULA
Harihari
Mt Hutt
Leeston
Lake
Ellesmere
Akaroa
Franz Josef Glacier
Mt Cook
3764
MOUNT
COOK
NAT. PARK
Rangitata
Mayfield
Canterbury
Bight
Fox Glacier
Bruce Bay
Mt Cook
(Hermitage)
Tasman
Glacier
Lake
Tekapo
Fairlie
Temuka
Haast
Lake
Pukaki
Timaru
Jackson Bay
Twizel
Makaroa
Lake
Benmore
Waimate
Wainono
Lagoon
Awarua
Point
Mt Aspiring
3027
Lake
Wanaka
Omarama
Waitaki
Kurow
Oamaru
MT ASPIRING
NATIONAL
PARK
Wanaka
Tarras
Ranfurly
Milford Sound
3265
Arrowtown
Cromwell
Hyde
Palmerston
Milford
Sound
Queenstown
Alexandra
Blueskin Bay
George Sound
Lake
Wakatipu
Kingston
Roxburgh
Clarks
Junction
Mosgiel
Dunedin
Caswell Sound
Lake
Te Anau
Mt Lyall
1905
1968
Edievale
Secretary
Island
Te Anau
Mossburn
Lumsden
Balclutha
Molyneux Bay
Doubtful Sound
Manapouri
Gore
Clinton
FIORDLAND
NATIONAL
PARK
Winton
Edendale
Owaka
Resolution
Island
Tuatapere
Riverton
Invercargill
Tokanui
Dusky Sound
Te
Waewae
Bay
Bluff
Chalky Inlet
Foveaux Strait
Halfmoon Bay
Paterson Inlet
Mason Bay
Stewart
Island
Southwest
Cape
Pacific
Ocean

orientation

Introduction

New Zealand's geography, while providing scenes of unsurpassed beauty, poses some difficulties for the independent traveller. There is an abundance of diversity in the landscape, but New Zealand is both long, thin and rough hewn, and also split into two main islands, making travelling time often longer than you expect. The bottom-line is that when your vacation time is short, it is impossible to see everything the country has to offer.

This selection of itineraries is designed to introduce you quickly and efficiently to some of New Zealand's most spectacular sights, and covers both the North and South islands. For this purpose, the 18 itineraries focus on five main hubs – chosen because of the range of attractions they offer as well as their easy accessibility. These hubs are: Auckland, whose international airport is the country's principal gateway; Rotorua, a hot springs wonderland in the central North Island; Wellington, New Zealand's capital city; Christchurch, the South Island's principal gateway; and Queenstown, the beautiful lakeside resort area in the lower part of the South Island.

Full-day, mainly walking itineraries guide you to the best of each of these locations. However, these centres offer only a part of the 'New Zealand experience'. To guide you through the rest of the country, a selection of half-day, full-day and multi-day driving itineraries have been included. These optional tours get you away from the hubs, to see some of the glory and diversity of the outlying countryside. They include visits to the historic Bay of Islands, the beautiful beaches of Coromandel, the adventure activities of Lake Taupo, the wineries of Wairarapa, the stunning glaciers of the West Coast of the South Island and the majesty of Milford Sound in Fiordland.

Getting Around

With so much natural beauty around and a good network of roads, it makes sense to rent a car and drive *(see pages 90–91)*. If time is a premium, travel to the main city hubs by domestic flights and save your driving for regional attractions. If not pressed for time, take a leisurely drive along New Zealand's long and winding roads and discover the country at your own pace.

Whether you're in New Zealand for just a few days or a week or more, this guide is invaluable. If you stay longer, the itineraries in this guide can be linked together for an extensive north to south or south to north tour of the whole country. Itinerary 10 takes you across the Cook Strait from the North Island to the South Island or vice versa, depending which way you're heading.

Left: Milford Sound, South Island
Right: all ready to hit the road

Auckland
& Environs

1. AUCKLAND'S HIGHLIGHTS *(see map below)*

A full-day itinerary taking in sights like Queen Street, the Auckland Domain, Parnell, Albert Park and the Sky Tower. A couple of short taxi rides are recommended to spare your feet as well as save some time along the way. Note: if the weather is inclement, the Auckland Explorer Bus (tel: 09 571 3119; www.explorerbus.co.nz) can take you on a hop-on/hop-off tour of many of the sights on this and the next itinerary. The bus starts at Ferry Building from 9am onwards.

Begin your tour downtown with breakfast at Viaduct Harbour – Mecca (85 Customs St West; tel: 09 358 1093) has plenty of options and good coffee – followed by a walk around the waterfront venue that, until recently, hosted the famous America's Cup yachting regatta. Take note of any restaurants or bars you like the look of as you may wish to return to spend your evenings there.

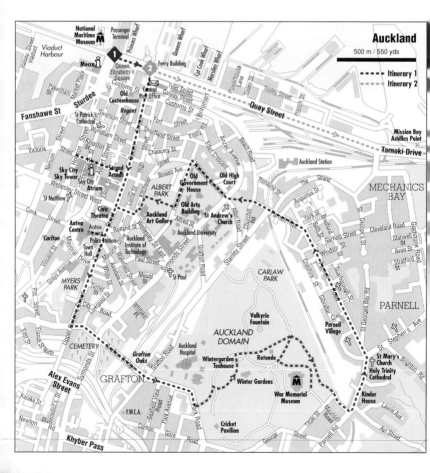

Auckland is New Zealand's largest city, containing within its urban sprawl more than a quarter of the country's entire population. What draws people here, as it has for centuries, is the combination of warm sub-tropical climate and the bountiful twin harbours of Waitemata and Manukau. Between the two harbours is an isthmus dotted with extinct volcanoes.

Exit Viaduct Harbour at the Quay Street archway, where a large suspended yacht is on display, a legacy of New Zealand's America's Cup endeavours. If you're interested in New Zealand's maritime history, check out the **New Zealand National Maritime Museum** (daily 9am–5pm; admission fee; tel: 09 373 0800; www.nzmaritime.org). Otherwise, go straight to the **Visitor Information Centre** (137 Quay Street) to pick up any maps that you may need, then walk on to the historic **Ferry Building** (*see page 27*). Cross Quay Street at this point, and you will be next to the Britomart train terminus and at the base of **Queen Street** – and the city's central shopping area.

Stroll along Queen Street, occasionally venturing down some of the side streets to explore more boutique shops. Further up on Queen Street, you will pass, on your right, the renowned department store, Smith & Caughey's (253 Queen Street) and the **Civic Theatre** (corner of Queen Street and Wellesley Street). The latter is a historic entertainment venue that hosts some of Auckland's premier events. Just beyond the Civic Theatre, you will find **Sky City Metro** (297 Queen Street), which houses the **Village Hoyts movie complex**; this is where the latest blockbusters are screened. There is also a Borders bookstore in the building.

The adjacent **Aotea Square** has several points of interest. The first is the Maori **Waharoa** (gateway): elaborately carved as a symbolic entrance to the square, it stands in stark contrast to the mirrored glass buildings around it. Across Aotea Square is Auckland's main cultural venue, **Aotea Centre** (tel: 09 309 2677; www.the-edge.co.nz). Walk across and browse in the foyer to see if the centre is hosting any events of interest to you. On Fridays and Saturdays between 10am and 5pm, the **Aotea Square Market** comes alive with stalls selling funky streetwear, jewellery, food and assorted bric-a-brac. City Council buildings border the square, with the most interesting being the renovated **Town Hall**: you'll recognise it by its angular shape and clock tower on the eastern fringe. After a good look around, hail a taxi to go to the Auckland War Memorial Museum. The journey of about 1km (½ mile) will take you over Grafton Bridge and past Auckland Hospital into **Auckland Domain**, New Zealand's oldest park.

The Domain was the site of a huge volcanic explosion which took place thousands of years ago, leaving features on the landscape still visible today. The wide crater has formed a natural amphitheatre arching from the hospital to the War Memorial Museum and is the venue of numerous outdoor sporting and cultural events. Ask the taxi driver to point out the Winter Gardens and Wintergarden Teahouse along the way.

Right: St Patrick's Day Parade, Aotea Square

Auckland War Memorial Museum

It is difficult to miss the **Auckland War Memorial Museum** (daily 10am–5pm; donation; tel: 09 307 7067; www.akmuseum.org.nz), with its dramatic features and a prime location that offers panoramic views of the rest of the Domain and parts of the city and harbour. As you walk around the museum, try to pick out the **One Tree Hill**, a volcanic cone that features in a song by Irish rock band U2 and which was once topped by a lone summit pine, but is now marked only by an obelisk. Note also the names of locations etched in the stone around the entire museum façade: these were the battlefields where New Zealanders were killed in overseas wars in the 20th century.

The museum was built in 1929 and an extension is currently being added that will expand the breadth of the museum's exhibits. Already, it is an excellent place for familiarising oneself with the natural, cultural and social history of New Zealand. For the first-time visitor, it is most valuable for the superb introduction to Maori culture: you can view artefacts such as a raised storehouse, a carved meeting house and, possibly the most spectacular exhibit, the **Te Toki a Tapiri**, the last of the great Maori war canoes, with its hull carved out of a single Totara log. The 25-m (82-ft) long canoe, built in 1836, could carry some 100 warriors. In addition, there are daily performances of the Maori song and dance, and the Scars on the Heart display tells the compelling story of New Zealand at war.

There is a café in the museum if you want a quick snack, but a better experience can be had if you walk from the front of the museum back down to the **Wintergarden Teahouse** (daily 9am–5pm). This is a lovely setting for a morning tea, and you will have views over duck ponds and meandering walkways. You should also consider visiting the **Winter Gardens** (daily 10am–4pm; free). This is a conservatory behind the tearooms, housing some 10,000 exotic plants. Look out in particular for the short native bush walk that will give you an introduction to the type of bush that still covers large parts of the country.

From the teahouse, follow the path that runs south-east around the perimeter of the Domain and all the way out to Parnell Road. This will eventually lead to the pretty shopping and eating inner-city suburb of **Parnell**. The walk will take about 15 to 20 minutes.

Along Parnell Road you will pass, on your

Above: lush Auckland Domain
Right: War Memorial Museum

auckland

right, **St Mary's Church** and the newer **Holy Trinity Cathedral**. The former is regarded as one of the finest wooden Gothic buildings in the world. Just 30m (33yds) further, at the corner with St Stephens Avenue, you will be greeted by a mixture of bakeries, 'dairies' (small grocery stores), fish-and-chip shops and the start of the designer shops that become more apparent just a little further down.

The **Parnell Village** complex on the left side of Parnell Road comprises a collection of wooden villas reclaimed and restored for retail purposes. Explore the myriad shops by ambling around the verandahs and over the little bridges linking villa to villa.

For lunch and to watch the world go by, get a seat under the awning at **Verve Café** (311 Parnell Road; tel: 09 379 2860). And if you are looking for special souvenirs, the **Höglund Art Glass Gallery** on 285 Parnell Road (tel: 09 300 6238) has stunning New Zealand hand-blown contemporary and classic crystal art glass by Ola and Marie Höglund.

Back to the City Centre

After thoroughly investigating Parnell, you have the choice of a half-hour walk back to the central city or of taking a taxi. Your ultimate destination is the landmark Sky Tower, for views over the whole city of Auckland and its surrounds.

If you are walking, veer left down Parnell Rise. When you have reached the bottom of this road, walked under the rail bridge and crossed the Grafton motorway extension, take a deep breath because you are now going up the other side again. A path leads from Churchill Road up through a reserve area to the junction of Symonds Street and Alten Road, where the Presbyterian **St Andrews** church stands with its Romanesque columns. Opposite the church is a low fence signalling the lower grounds of Auckland University.

Cross over, head west along the Waterloo Quadrant and you will see the old **High Court** on your right, with its historic older chamber and court rooms joined to a modern extension. Work started on the old Court building in 1865 and the first sitting took place three years later. The carved stone heads and gargoyles which adorn the exterior of the court were crafted by Anton Teutenburg, a Prussian immigrant who was paid 15 shillings a day for the task.

Moving on, the **Old Government House** is on your left at 12 Princes Street. Cross the road to the entrance and take a stroll through the grounds, now owned by the university. The building appears to be stone, though in fact its exterior cladding is all kauri, the wood of the tall coniferous tree which once dominated the New Zealand bush. Walk along beside the building and enjoy some of the dense gardens on the hillside leading up to Princes Street.

Make your way up Princes Street, dominated by the **Old Arts Building** on your left, which was designed and built with the help of students from Auckland University College and opened in 1926. Locals call it The Wedding Cake because of its ornate pinnacled white-stone construction.

Right: Parnell Street shops

Albert Park and the Waterfront

Opposite the Old Arts Building is **Albert Park**, a beautifully maintained inner city sanctum featuring a floral clock, statues of Queen Victoria and Sir George Grey (1812–1898), a strong and influential early leader of colonial New Zealand, a band rotunda and hordes of students lazing on the grass.

Take one of the paths that lead downhill to Kitchener Street, and on the southern corner with Wellesley Street is the **Main Gallery** of the **Auckland Art Gallery**. Through a courtyard across the street is its younger sibling, the **New Gallery** (both daily 10am–5pm; free; www.aucklandartgallery.govt.nz; tel: 09 379 1349). The former displays mainly historical and European art collections while the latter is a showcase for cutting-edge contemporary art.

Make a stop to view the exhibits, then continue into Wellesley Street just a short distance away and turn right. You are right back in the heart of Auckland – Queen Street.

To end your exploration of the central city, walk a block down Queen Street towards the sea to Victoria Street, then turn left and walk up the slope to Auckland's most prominent landmark, the **Sky Tower** (daily 8.30am till late; admission fee; tel: 09 363 6000; www.skytower.co.nz). At 328m (360yd) high, it is the tallest tower in the southern hemisphere, offering breathtaking views for more than 80km (50 miles) in every direction. If the standard outlook from the viewing level is not enough, you might want to consider taking on the **Vertigo** (daily 9am–7pm; tel: 09 368 1917; www.4vertigo.com), a 2-hour guided tour up the inside of the mast, culminating in a 15-minute internal climb from the upper observation deck to the first crow's nest. At this point, you have the option of another way down the tower with the **Sky Jump** (daily 10am–6pm; tel: 09 368 1839; www.skyjump.co.nz), a wire-controlled 192-m (630-ft) upright fall from a platform near the viewing area.

Rebo Café & Bar (daily 24 hours), located at the ground level of the adjacent **SKYCITY**, offers a good view of the 'sky jumpers' touching down. The **SKYCITY casinos** (daily 24 hours; www.skycityauckland.co.nz), with its various bars, entertainment and gaming areas, offers – if you are game – a bit of fun with which to wind up Itinerary 1.

2. AROUND AUCKLAND'S BAYS *(see map, p22)*

A half-day driving itinerary around the bays of Auckland's spectacular waterfront, with the option of ending the day at Devonport. Drive alongside the Waitemata Harbour to Kelly Tarlton's Antarctic Encounter and Underwater World. Take a further break at Mission Bay, and then continue to Achilles Point for views back over the harbour and the Hauraki Gulf. To make this a full day trip, take the Fullers Ferry across the harbour to the North Shore suburb of Devonport.

Auckland's dominant feature is its sparkling harbour – the Waitemata – and this itinerary gives you a fabulous opportunity to experience it. Start at the Ferry Building on Quay Street.

The **Ferry Building** on Queen Street, where you start your drive, is one of Auckland's best-known landmarks. Built in 1912, the building is still the focal point for commuter ferries that link Auckland with the North Shore and the islands of Waitemata Harbour. Continue driving east along Quay Street, keeping the port on your left. This will lead to **Tamaki Drive**, where you will pass the container terminal and Hobson Bay on your left and **Parnell Baths**, an outdoor swimming complex, on your right. The most prominent feature across the Waitemata Harbour is the volcanic cone of Rangitoto Island. Rangitoto means 'blood-red sky', so named by the Maori following an eruption; the summit is 260m (864ft) high. The volcano is now dormant and the island a bush-clad reserve. The island is accessible by ferry, and summit walks can also be organised (for details on ferry schedule and rates, contact Fullers Cruise Centre, tel: 09 367 9111; www.fullers.co.nz).

Contrasting with Rangitoto's natural serenity is the human influence all along State Highway (SH) 77. Views of the harbour are highly sought after and the houses in this area command premium prices. Following the route, with signposts to St Heliers, you will pass the first of many city beaches along the way, starting with **Okahu Bay**. On your right is the extensive grassed area of **Orakei Domain**.

Kelly Tarlton's

As you drive around the bay, watch out for **Hammerhead Restaurant** (19 Tamaki Drive, tel: 09 521 4400), a large seafood eatery on your right with good views of the harbour. Use it as a landmark to move into the right-hand lane and ease off the accelerator as just beyond the restaurant, at 23 Tamaki Drive, is your first leg-stretch at **Kelly Tarlton's Antarctic Encounter and Underwater World** (daily 9am–8pm summer, 9am–6pm winter; admission fee; tel: 09 528 0603; www.kellytarltons.co.nz).

When it was opened in 1985, Kelly Tarlton's was the first aquarium of its kind in the world. Built under the sea, special acrylic tunnels take you through holding tanks of exotic New Zealand marine life. The complex was recently expanded to include a journey in special 'snow cats' for a taste of the

Left: Auckland's landmark Sky Tower and Harbour Bridge
Above: the Ferry Building

Kelly Tarlton's
Antarctic Encounter
Underwater World

Antarctic wilds. The heated vehicles plunge through a fierce white-out storm to emerge in the tranquil beauty of a recreated Antarctic landscape. You could easily spend an hour in each section of Kelly Tarlton's, so plan sufficient time for it.

Mission Bay and Beaches

Resume your journey east for another 1km (½ mile) until you arrive at **Mission Bay**. Turn left off Tamaki Drive into the first public car-parking area, or the second area near the large clock. For a drink and a snack, try **Mecca** (85 Tamaki Drive; daily 7am–late; tel: 09 528 0017), which has a superb setting in an old stone building within the park grounds. Alternatively, you can have a picnic on the lawn leading to the beach, with supplies obtained from one of the delicatessens or bakeries on the other side of the road.

Take a walk along the promenade, settle yourself on the sand, or paddle in the sea. If you are feeling energetic, try the walk around the remaining two bays, **Kohimarama** and **St Heliers**. The seaside walk is just under 2km (1¼ miles) to Kohimarama and a further 1km (½ mile) to St Heliers. Once a year, this route is filled with tens of thousands of people who take to the road in the popular 'Round the Bays' fun run. If you are in your car, drive up Cliff Road at the end of Tamaki Drive to Ladies Bay and the lookout at Achilles Point. A commemorative plaque is placed here in honour of HMS Achilles, which took part in the 1939 Battle of the River Plate. From here, retrace your path along Tamaki Drive and return to the Ferry Building. If you would like to do a bit of shopping, follow Quay Street around past Viaduct Harbour for 1km (½ mile), turning left at the start of Victoria Park and then first right into Victoria Street West. The big red-brick chimney signals the **Victoria Park Market** (daily 9am–6pm), where craft shops and cafés abound.

Devonport

If you have a few hours to spare, catching a ferry from downtown across to historic Devonport is a pleasant option. Ferries at the Fullers Cruise Centre run every half hour and the crossing takes just 10 to 12 minutes.

From the Devonport ferry terminal, stroll up **Victoria Street**, the main street. Situated just next to the landmark **Esplanade Hotel** is the **Visitor Information Centre** (Mon–Fri 8am–5pm, Sat–Sun 8.30am–5pm; tel: 09 446 0677). If the weather is good, you may wish to ask about walking options to Mt Victoria, North Head or Cheltenham Beach for great harbour and gulf views. Alternatively, you could browse in the antique stores or watch life go by from one of the cafés, such as **Mecca Esplanade** on 1 Victoria Road (tel: 09 445 9559).

Left: browse at Victoria Park Market

3. BAY OF ISLANDS *(see map, p30)*

A 2- or 3-day trip to a picturesque bay in the north. Travel via Warkworth and Whangarei to Paihia. Take a cruise to the famous Hole in the Rock and spend the night at Russell. Visit Haruru Falls and the historic Waitangi Treaty House on your way back to Auckland.

Begin this trip out of Auckland from opposite the Ferry Building on Quay Street. Head west, following the signs over the Harbour Bridge. Continue on along SH1 north, following the signs to Whangarei.

The **Bay of Islands**, a maritime park of some 144 islands and bays, is some 241km (150 miles) north of Auckland and located midway in a peninsula known as Northland. The Bay of Islands is an area of notable firsts in New Zealand's history. It was the legendary landing place of Polynesian explorer Kupe in the 10th century; Captain Cook sheltered in the bays and gave the area its name in 1769; New Zealand's first European colonists settled in Russell; the Treaty of Waitangi, New Zealand's founding document, was signed here; Russell was the nation's first capital – the list goes on. But first you have to get up early to enjoy it. Leave Auckland at about 7am as the drive north can take up to 4 hours, depending on traffic flow and stops en route.

Journey to Paihia

A good breakfast spot to stop over is **Warkworth**, just under an hour from Auckland in an area known as the **Kowhai Coast**. Try the **Bridge House Lodge** (16 Elizabeth Street; tel: 09 425 8351) by the bridge for breakfast, and stretch your legs with a walk by the picturesque Mahurangi River.

Driving another 100km (62 miles) will bring you to Northland's main city, **Whangarei**. An information centre on your left on SH1 (Tarewa Park) as you enter the city has good facilities including a café. Follow the signs to Kawakawa, which takes about an hour from Whangarei, and then look for the turn-off to Paihia via Opua. There is plenty to do in **Paihia**, a neat little town with hotels, restaurants and modest nightlife. However, be warned that in summer, the beautiful bays, beaches and history combine to make this harbourside resort a tourist magnet, with accommodation sometimes hard to find.

Hole in the Rock

Go to the Maritime Building in Paihia where the **Bay of Islands Information Office** (daily 8am–5pm; tel: 09 402 7683; www.northland.org.nz) is located and pick up some brochures. Recommended is the **Hole in the Rock** cruise with **Kings Dolphin Cruises and Tours** (Maritime Building, tel: 09 402 8288; www.kings-tours.co.nz). The 3-hour trip through this peculiar geographical feature departs at 9.15am and 1.35pm and includes a Maori welcome or *pohwhiri*, dolphin watching and a full commentary on local myths and legends. If you want something a little quicker try the **Mack-Attack**, a 90-minute blast to the Hole in the Rock in a powerful boat capable of travelling up to speeds of 50 knots.

On your way back from the cruise either get dropped off across the harbour in **Russell** – where New Zealand's first white colonialists settled – or take the regular ferry there that departs from the Maritime Building. Russell, once known as 'the hell hole of the Pacific' and famous for its unruly population of whalers and runaways, is now a quiet town with a distinct Victorian atmosphere. Walk down the waterfront and seek out **Pompallier House** (daily 10am–5pm), a Catholic mission house dating back to 1841. Also make time to visit **Russell Museum** (daily 10am–4pm) along York Street. Good options for accommodation include the historic **Duke of Marlborough Hotel** (tel: 09 403 7829; www.theduke.co.nz) or, back at Paihia and set within the Waitangi National Reserve, the **Copthorne Hotel and Resort** (Tau Henare Drive; tel: 09 402 7411; www.copthorne-bay-of-islands.nz-hotels.com).

From Paihia, two 'must-sees' are **Haruru Falls** and the Waitangi Treaty House. To get to the falls, once the location of New Zealand's first river port, follow the signs from the bridge leading to the Waitangi National Reserve (3km/2 miles from Paihia).

A more adventurous way of experiencing the power of the falls is by kayak. Half- and full-day guided tours leaving from Waitangi Beach explore the Waitangi Estuary and its mangrove forest and visit the Haruru Falls (contact **Coastal Kayakers**, tel: 09 402 8105; www.coastalkayakers.co.nz).

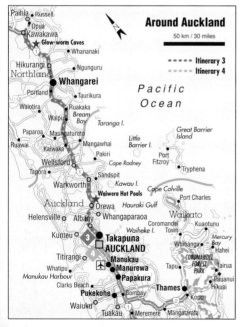

Around Auckland
50 km / 30 miles

- - - - Itinerary 3
- - - - Itinerary 4

Pacific Ocean

Above right: Waitangi Treaty House
Right: Hahei beach, Coromandel

Waitangi Treaty House

After viewing the falls, retrace your route and follow the signs to the **Waitangi National Reserve** (daily 9am–5pm; tel: 09 402 7437; www.waitangi.net.nz). Allow at least an hour to stroll the grounds and view the Maori meeting house, Maori war canoe and the **Waitangi Treaty House**, where New Zealand's founding document was signed in 1840. Have lunch at the stylish **Waikokopu Café**, located in the Treaty House grounds.

You can either return to Auckland, or carry on north for 223 km (140 miles) to **Cape Reinga**. The Twin Coast Highway will take you to the top of North Island and back down a west coast route to Auckland. If returning direct to Auckland, stop by the **Waiwera Infinity Thermal Resort** (daily 9.30am–10pm; tel: 09 427 8800; www.waiwera.co.nz), 47km (29 miles) north of the city and relax those tired muscles with a soak in the hot mineral pools.

4. COROMANDEL PENINSULA *(see map, p30)*

A multi-day itinerary visiting the former gold-rush town of Thames, then over the Coromandel Ranges to the resort area of Pauanui and Tairua. Relax at Hot Water and Hahei beaches, then either return to Auckland or continue to Rotorua, your next hub.

Thames, the gateway to the Coromandel Peninsula, is an easy 90-minute drive from Auckland. Start on Queen Street and drive up to Karangahape Road; turn left then veer right before Grafton Bridge following the signs on to SH1.

Follow SH1 south for about 20km (12½ miles) and just after the Bombay Hills, take the turn-off for SH2, sign-posted to Tauranga. Follow the highway another 50km (31 miles) before you turn east on to SH25, sign-posted

to **Thames**. The road heads out across the low-lying former swamp-lands of the **Hauraki Plains**. Over 1000km (620 miles) of drains and canals have turned this land into productive dairy pasture, though it is still prone to occasional flooding.

Take care as you approach the **Kopu Bridge**, which spans the **Waihou River**. It is a long one-lane bridge controlled by traffic lights so make sure you wait until the lights are green. It is not the last one-lane bridge you will come across while driving in this region so stay alert, make sure you slow down, and follow the road signs that indicate who gives way to whom. A short drive beyond the bridge and SH25 comes to a T-junction at the base of the Coromandel Ranges. Turn left and drive 5km (3 miles), following the signs to Thames.

Things to do at Thames

At the turn of the 20th century, thanks to its gold mines, Thames had the largest population in New Zealand, with around 18,000 inhabitants and well over 100 hotels. The population today has trickled down to about 7,000.

Make your first stop the **Tourist Information Centre** – the teal green build-ing on the right as you enter the town at 206 Pollen Street (Mon–Fri 8.30am–5pm, Sat–Sun 9am–4pm; tel: 07 868 7284, www.thames-info.co.nz). Here you can get brochures and information on some of the activities in the region.

Drive down Pollen Street – the main street in Thames – and you will get a bit of a feel of how the town was in its gold mining hey-day. Some of the old buildings of the mining era remain, most notably the renovated **Brian Boru Hotel** at the corner of Richmond Street and Pollen Street (tel: 07 868 6523). It is a good place to either stay or have a drink at the end of the day.

Today, Thames acts as a service town for the rural community but what you should explore are the old gold mines. Follow Pollen Street north and

turn right, back on to SH25 and then turn quickly right again, across the traffic to the **Goldmine Experience** (daily 10am–4pm; tel: 07 868 8514; www.goldmine-experience.co.nz). The old site of the 1868 Gold Crown claim now features a photographic exhibition of Thames. The hosts, not surprisingly, are a mine of information and will take you, if you are not claustrophobic, on a short guided tour of an old mine shaft. This underground tour, which will take at least 40 minutes, can be muddy, especially during the wetter months, so go prepared with closed-toe footwear. For those who dislike being in con-fined dark spaces, there are alternative activities, including gold panning.

Above: Brian Boru Hotel
Left: Goldmine Experience. **Right:** Hot Water Beach

Pauanui and Tairua

After your exploration of Thames, resume your drive to the beautiful beaches of the peninsula's east coast. Head back 5km (3 miles) south of Thames to the SH25A turn-off, sign-posted to **Whangamata** and **Whitianga**. This 51-km (31½-mile) scenic route takes you through the scenic **Coromandel Forest Park**. SH25A joins SH25 on the other side of the Coromandel Ranges. At the settlement of Hikuai, which is marked by a solitary petrol station, turn right, taking the road to Pauanui 15km (9 miles) further on.

Pauanui is a renowned playground for wealthy Aucklanders and features a beautiful beach at the base of the Pauanui headland. Book into somewhere in this area for a couple of nights and use it as your base from which to explore. If you want a real treat, stay at the **Mercure Grand Puka Park Resort** (tel: 07 864 8088; www.pukapark.co.nz), with its Pacific-style chalets nestled among the ferns and bush behind the main settlement. Stay as long as you wish in Pauanui. Swim at the beach; try some bush walks, go kayaking, fishing or diving or play a round of golf. It can all be done from either Pauanui or the older, but no less beautiful, settlement of **Tairua**, across the Tairua Harbour.

Hot Water and Other Beaches

A full-day trip that you must do involves a drive north 50km (31 miles) from Pauanui through Tairua, turning right at **Whenuakite** and following the signs to **Hot Water Beach**. Aim to arrive around low tide time (your hotel, or the Visitor Information Centre at the Pauanui Service Station on Vista Paku Road, will be able to advise you on the tides). Hire a spade at the Hot Water Beach shop, and stroll along the beach to where you can dig a hole in the sand and wallow in the soothing hot spring waters until the tide comes back in.

Make time for a visit to **Hahei**, 10km (6 miles) further north – my favourite beach on the peninsula. You can rent a kayak for a guided trip to the stunning **Cathedral Cove** with **Cathedral Cove Kayaks** (tel: 07 866 3877; www.seakayaktours.co.nz), or take the short drive north following the signs near the shops to a lookout. From here are breathtaking views of **Mercury Bay**. If you have time, there are several sign-posted walks you can take from the lookout right down to Cathedral Cove.

Head back from Hahei and drive 11km (7 miles) to **Cook's Beach** and **Flaxmill Bay**. A good place for a snack is the **Eggsentric Café and Restaurant** at 1047 Purangi Road (tel: 07 866 0307) on the left just after Flaxmill Bay. Drive another 1km (¾ mile) along the road and park near the ferry landing. The ferry will take you on a short trip across the inlet to **Whitianga** where you can visit the museum opposite the wharf or wander around the town and visit craft shops. Consider dinner at **On the Rocks**, overlooking Mercury Bay at 20 The Esplanade (tel: 07 866 4833) before making the return journey on the ferry to your car.

Continue to Rotorua

From here, you can return to your base in Auckland, perhaps via a scenic route around the top of the peninsula. This adds two hours to the journey, but it can be broken with a stay in the charming **Coromandel Town** on the north-west coast. **Anchor Lodge Motel** on 448 Wharf Road (tel: 07 866 7992; www.anchorlodgecoromandel.co.nz) is a good place to stay at. Alternatively, you can also combine this itinerary with the next hub, Rotorua. To do so, drive 34km (21 miles) south on SH25 to the popular summer beach resort of **Whangamata**, after which it is a straightforward 100-km (62-mile) journey through **Waihi** and on to SH2 to **Tauranga**. From here, it's another 86km (53½ miles) to **Rotorua**. Follow SH2 east through Te Puke and then veer south on SH33 instead of carrying on to Whakatane. SH33 will take you past Lake Rotoiti and the eastern shore of Lake Rotorua before you reach Rotorua proper – your base for the next few days.

Rotorua & *Environs*

5. ROTORUA'S HIGHLIGHTS *(see maps, p36 and p38)*

A full-day driving and walking itinerary of Rotorua. Take the Skyline Gondola for a view over Rotorua. Visit the Whakarewarewa Thermal Area and take a scenic drive to the Blue and Green Lakes. See the Buried Village, then return to Rotorua for a dip at the Polynesian Pools. Round off the night with a Maori concert party and a *hangi* meal.

Your day begins at the Tourism Rotorua Visitor Information Office at 1167 Fenton Street (daily 8am–5pm, till 6pm during summer; tel: 07 348 5179; www.rotoruanz.com). Pick up some useful information and maps from the office, and book in advance for a variety of activities.

Rotorua, as the locals proudly boast, is the only place in New Zealand where you can tell exactly where you are with your eyes closed. They are referring, of course, to the distinctive aroma of sulphur that permeates the town, courtesy of its boiling mud pools and hot springs. To visit Rotorua with your eyes shut would be a travesty, however, because it is an area of rich cultural and scenic beauty. Block your nose, and head out boldly.

Leave at about 9am, or else you may miss the 10.30am farm show at Rainbow Farm later on. Head west on Arawa Street, then turn right on to Ranolf Street (the start of SH5). The drive takes you past **Kuirau Park** on your left, a 25-ha (62-acre) reserve. Drive on, and along Fairy Springs Road about 4½km (3 miles) out from the city, aim for the **Skyline Skyrides** gondola (daily 9am–8pm; admission fee; tel: 07 347 0027; www.skylineskyrides.co.nz).

The Skyline is on your left and there is ample parking, so pull off the road, buy a ticket and in minutes the 900-m (2,953-ft) lift, with a vertical rise of 200m (656ft) takes you up the slopes of **Mt Ngongotaha** for a panoramic view. Stroll around and gaze over the region you will soon be exploring.

Rainbow Farm and Springs

Half-an-hour or so and it's time to ride back down either on the gondola or the luge, a three-wheel cart, on the exciting 1-km (¾ mile) long track. Just 100m (110yds) down the road is **Rainbow Farm** on your right and **Rainbow Springs** (both open daily 8am–5pm; admission fee; tel: 07 347 9301; www.rainbow nz.co.nz) on your left. Park by the springs and follow the signs leading you

Left: Mercury Bay, Coromandel Peninsula
Right: teeth inspection time – Rainbow Farm

under the road to the farm. Every day at 10.30am (and also at 11.45am, 1, 2.30 and 4pm), a special show introduces visitors to New Zealand's farming heritage. Efficient and strapping farm lads take you through the finer points of mustering and shearing sheep, and a range of other farm activities.

After strolling around the farm viewing farm animals and a kiwifruit display, take the path back under the road to your next Rotorua experience. The ticket you bought earlier also gives you access to **Rainbow Springs**, which boasts more than 150 species of native New Zealand fauna spread over picturesque grounds. Join up with a guide who will introduce you to pools of clear water alive with rainbow and brown trout, among other attractions.

It takes 1–2 hours to tour Rainbow Springs. Then, get into your car and follow SH5 back towards town, taking the turn-off for Lake Road. Park the car in the lakefront parking area near the jetty. Every day at 12.30pm the *Lakeland Queen*, a 22-m (72-ft) paddle steamer takes passengers around **Lake Rotorua** on a lunchtime cruise (tel: 07 348 6634, www.lakelandqueen.co.nz). On board, you will be entertained with the love story of Hinemoa and Tutanekai – a Maori legend of Romeo and Juliet proportions, but fortunately with a happy ending.

If you miss the boat, or choose not to sail, 50m (55yds) to your left (facing the lake) is the **Lakeside Café and Crafts Shop** (tel: 07 349 2626). Have lunch here and check out its selection of crafts for sale.

Sights Along Lake Rotorua

You can, and should, also walk north-west from the café along the narrow driveway that heads past the **Rotorua Yacht Club** around the lake-front to **St Faith's Church** and **Ohinemutu**. This tiny village on the lake-front was the main settlement when the first Europeans arrived in the 1800s. The settlement is renowned for the idyllic setting of the church, built in 1885. There

is a beautiful stained glass window in the church, and another notable feature is the etched window depicting a Maori Jesus Christ.

With the lake as a backdrop, the etched window creates the illusion of Christ walking on water. Another more curious feature of Ohinemutu is the raised graves around the church, made necessary by the thermal activity beneath the ground. Several years ago, a Rotorua resident had a fright when his toilet exploded due to thermal activity heating up water in his pipes.

After strolling the lake-front, return to your car and head to town for some shopping. Leading directly south from the park area at the lake-front is **Tutanekai Street**,

Rotorua's main drag. There are a wide variety of shops, though not particularly spectacular, and more eating options. Parking is easy to find all along the street. Return to your car and drive east on Pukaki Street past the Convention Centre and into the **Government Gardens**.

On its grounds, the **Rotorua Museum of Art and History** (daily 9.30am–5pm; admission fee; tel: 07 349 4350; www.rotoruanz.com) is well worth a visit. The distinctive 1908 Tudor-style building is home to artefacts from Rotorua's past and recounts the romantic history of the famous Pink and White Terraces *(see page 38)* and also the history of the Te Arawa tribe.

Whakarewarewa and the Coloured Lakes

Sometime now you should practise trying to pronounce the name of your next destination, **Whakarewarewa** (say far-car-rear-wah-rear-wah) – the closest thermal resort to the city. To get there head back to Fenton Street and turn left. Just 3km (1½ miles) south and on your left is the **New Zealand Maori Arts and Crafts Institute** (daily 8am–5pm; admission fee; tel: 07 348 9047; www.nzmaori.co.nz) where you can watch skilled Maori carvers and flax weavers at work. The area surrounding the institute has extensive thermal activity ranging from bubbling mud pools and boiling springs to the famous **Pohutu Geyser** which erupts up to a height of 30m (98ft). Allow at least 90 minutes to explore this area and the adjacent **Whakarewarewa Thermal Village** (daily 8.30am–5pm; admission fee; tel: 07 349 3463; www.whakarewarewa.com).

From Whakarewarewa, it is a scenic drive to the mysterious lakes. To get there, drive back up Fenton Street towards town, turn right into Sala Street just by the Grand Tiara Hotel; follow the street out to Te Ngae Road (SH30) and then turn off on the first main road to your right – Tarawera Road. About 10km (6 miles) from the city, along the forest-fringed Tarawera Road, you suddenly drop down to the beautiful sight of **Lake Tikitapu**, or the **Blue Lake**. Have a dip in the lake or else hire a canoe or pedal boat from the Blue Lake Holiday Park just up behind the road.

Continuing, the road rises to a crest and a vantage point from which you see both Lake Tikitapu, and the larger

Above: Rotorua Museum of Art and History
Right: Sliding into Blue Lake

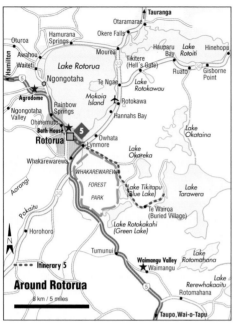

Tauranga
Otaramarae
Oturoa   Hamurana   Okere Falls
          Springs
Awahou   Haparu Lake   Hinehopu
Waiteti   *Lake Rotorua*   Bay Rotoiti
          Ngongotaha   Tikitere Ruato   Gisborne
                        (Hell's Gate)   Point
Hamilton   Te Ngae   Lake
Agrodome   Rotokawau
        Mokoia   Rotokawa
Ngongotaha Rainbow *Island*
Valley Springs
        Ohinemutu   Hannahs Bay
Bath House   Lake
Rotorua   Owhata   Okataina
          Lynmore
                  Lake
Whakarewarewa   Okareka
        WHAKAREWAREWA
Aorangi FOREST   Lake Tikitapu   Lake
        PARK   (Blue Lake)   Tarawera
Pokaitu   Te Wairoa
                (Buried Village)
        Horohoro   Lake Rotokakahi
                (Green Lake)
        Tumunui   Lake
N   Waimangu Valley Rotomahana
                ★ Waimangu
■ ■ ■ **Itinerary 5**   Lake
                    Rerewhakaaitu
Around Rotorua   Rotomahana

8 km / 5 miles

                    Taupo, Wai-o-Tapu

Lake Rotokakahi, the **Green Lake**. This lake is not open for boating or swimming however, because it is *tapu* (sacred) to the local Maori. The road swings down around the edge of the lake, but gives you no access to the water.

Here you are following the historic tourist route opened in the 19th century to the former **Pink and White Terraces**, once known as the eighth wonder of the world. The naturally-formed silica terraces on the shores of **Lake Rotomahana** were like a giant staircase, with a fan-shaped edge spilling across almost 300m (328yds) of lake-front. But nature proved unkind to its own wonders, and now people follow the route to witness a tragedy. For on 10 June 1886, the massive volcanic eruption of Mount Tarawera obliterated the terraces and destroyed two Maori villages in the vicinity by burying them under a hail of ash and mud.

The Buried Village of Te Wairoa

A memorial to the tragedy is just a few minutes' drive past Lake Rotokakahi – the **Buried Village** excavation of Te Wairoa (daily 9am–4.30pm, till 5.30pm in summer; admission fee; tel: 07 362 8287; www.buriedvillage.co.nz). Turn right off Tarawera Road and into the carpark in front of the Buried Village souvenir shop and tea room. A marked walk takes you through the village excavations and sites including a Maori *whare* (house), a flour mill, blacksmith's shop, a store and a hotel. Soak in the surreal atmosphere of the village, watched over by the legacy of the early European settlers – a series of poplar and sycamore trees. Watch out for the *whare* where a Maori elder, who had foretold the tragedy, was trapped for four days before being rescued alive.

Another interesting exhibit is the front third of a large canoe believed to have been constructed by northern tribes for an attack on the Te Arawa of Rotorua in 1823. Depending on time, and energy levels, you can either make your way past an animal enclosure back to the entrance, or you can take the highly recommended but longer bush walk back. A track crosses Te Wairoa stream and leads steeply down through dense native bush to a waterfall and rapids. Continue on and you're back at the souvenir shop and tea rooms.

From Te Wairoa, it is a short drive further along the same main road to **Lake Tarawera**. You will first come to a lookout point, with **Mount Tarawera** looming across the lake in the distance. Then drop down to the waterfront and the Tarawera Landing, situated at a quiet little bay with a jetty.

Above Right: have a soak at the Polynesian Spa
Right: Maori-style entertainment

Have afternoon tea at the Landing Café right opposite the jetty. And if your timing is good take a scenic lake cruise (summer only, tel: 07 362 8595; departs daily at 1.30, 2.30 and 3.30pm). The café also prepares good evening meals if you are at the lake at the end of the day.

Spa Delights

Time to return to Rotorua. Follow the same route back out along Tarawera Road to Te Ngae Road which leads you back to Fenton Street. Turn right into Hinemoa Street for your next treat. To round off the evening, have a relaxing dip in the natural healing geothermal waters of the **Polynesian Spa** (daily 6.30am–11pm; admission fee; tel: 07 348 1328; www.polynesianspa.co.nz). The spa also offers a variety of massage treatments up till 6pm (bookings are essential).

Top off the night with a Maori *hangi* and cultural show at the **Tamaki Maori Village** (ticket office at the Tamaki Heritage Experiences Building, 1220 Hinemaru Street; tel: 07 346 2823; e-mail: tamaki@wave.co.nz; www. maoriculture.co.nz). For this tourism award-winning venture, guests are picked up for a 20-minute bus ride to a replica village in an atmospheric forest setting. During the ride, guides will introduce them to Maori culture, myths and legends. Guests will also have an opportunity to experience a *hangi*, which is the traditional Maori method of cooking food. Pork and vegetables are buried in the ground on top of red-hot stones and steam-cooked for hours. Join in the concert at the end of the evening and you may finish the night with a Maori *hongi* – a pressing of noses to signify friendship.

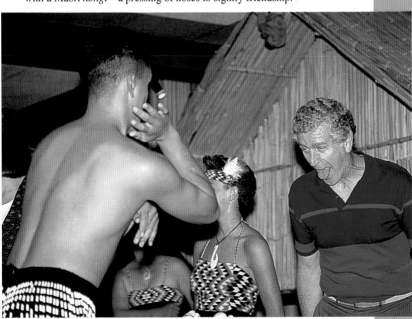

rotorua & environs

6. TAURANGA DISTRICT *(see map below)*

A day or half-day drive north of Rotorua through the kiwifruit grow-ing area of Te Puke to Mount Maunganui. A picnic at the beach and on to Tauranga.

Start at the Tourism Rotorua Visitor Information Office on Fenton Street. Follow SH30 out of town (via Te Ngae Road, left off Fenton Street as you head away from the lake) which circles around Lake Rotorua and takes you past the airport on what is now SH33. The highway veers inland away from the top end of Lake Rotorua and sweeps past Okawa Bay, providing some picturesque views of Lake Rotoiti.

The Tauranga district, if you haven't covered it in your drive from the Coro-mandel Peninsula, is an easy day trip from Rotorua (86km/53½ miles) along an inter-esting north-bound route. Make **Okere Falls**, at the head of Lake Rotoiti, your first stop of the day. Take the sharp left turn just past the Okere Falls shop and fol-low the signs to a small car park. This option takes you to the start of an easy 10-minute walk to a lookout directly above the **Kaituna River**.

Te Puke and Mt Maunganui

Continuing on by car from Okere Falls for about 25km (15½ miles), and watch for signs to **Longridge Park** (daily 9am–5pm; admission fee; www.funpark.co.nz; tel: 07 533 1515). The park is a unique attraction combining a relaxed drive through a genuine working farm and kiwifruit plantation. You can also try thrilling jet-boat rides or whitewater raft-ing on the upper reaches of the Kaituna River.

After Longridge Park and the small town of Paengaroa, the road joins up with SH2 leading to **Te Puke**, a kiwifruit growing area. Just past the turn-off to Whakatane you will see a giant kiwifruit marking the location of **Kiwifruit Country** (daily 9am–5pm; admission fee; tel: 07 573 6340; www.kiwifruitcountry.co.nz), a tourist attraction with, surprise, kiwifruit as its theme.

A roundabout 16km (10 miles) beyond Te Puke signals the approach of Tauranga and Mount Maunganui. Do not veer left on SH2, but continue on along what becomes Maunganui Road. Follow it about 4km (2½ miles) to reach **'The Mount'**. The major landmark is **Mount Maunganui** itself, a conical rocky feature rising

Above: Te Puke's claim to fame

to a height of 232m (761ft) above sea level. The Mount is of important historical significance as it was one of the largest locations of early Maori settlement in New Zealand.

The well sign-posted **Visitor Information Centre** on Salisbury Avenue, left off Maunganui Road (tel: 07 575 5099; www.nztauranga.com) can give you a leaflet to walking the Mount, and other useful information. Follow Salisbury Avenue around past the sheltered Pilot Bay to the base of the Mount, park near the Domain camp grounds, and follow signs to the start of the tracks. Depending on how energetic you feel, you can either take the **Summit Road Track** to the top of the Mount, or circle around the base.

Have a picnic on the beach at any one of the sheltered spots back on **Pilot Bay** or head the short distance north to **Marine Parade** and the sweeping **Mount Maunganui Beach**. Buy food from any of the inexpensive tea rooms and cafés back along Maunganui Road (which is walking distance from the Maunganui beach, behind Mount Drury Reserve).

On to Tauranga

After lunch, head into **Tauranga**, driving back along Maunganui Road, cutting a sharp right at the roundabout to head along SH29 (Hewletts Road) and over the harbour bridge. As you come off the bridge, follow the signs left at the roundabout to the city centre and park your car at **The Strand** near the railway station. Stroll to the north end of **Herries Park** and cross the road to see a ceremonial canoe, **Te Awanui**, on display.

A path at the base of the hill takes you through the pleasant Robbins Park and the Rose Garden and to the **Monmouth Military Redoubt**. British troops were stationed here during unrest in the 1860s and their earthworks and guns survive as reminders of the bloody conflict between Maori and Pakeha in this area in days done by.

Back along The Strand a walk brings you to the main shopping precinct and Devonport Road. **Mediterraneo** at No 62 (tel: 04 577 0487) is a good café stop for afternoon tea.

Back in the car, head up from The Strand two blocks to Cameron Road and turn left. A 3km (2 mile) drive will take you to 17th Avenue. Turn right for the **Compass Community Village** (Mon–Fri 8.30am–4.30pm and Sat–Sun 8am–4pm; admission fee; tel: 07 571 3700). The village features a variety of craft shops over its 6-ha (15-acre) complex.

Allow yourself about 90 minutes for the return journey to Rotorua. Turn right out of 17th Avenue into Cameron Road and drive 3½km (2½ miles). Turn left and just follow the signs to Te Puke, SH33, and on back to Rotorua.

Right: Mount Maunganui Beach

7. TAUPO *(see map, p40)*

An easy-paced day trip from Rotorua, heading south on SH5 to Huka Falls and Taupo. Cruise on New Zealand's largest lake and return to Rotorua via the Craters of the Moon. Alternatively, stay overnight and carry on your journey through to Wellington.

Start at the Tourism Rotorua Visitor Information Office on Fenton Street. Follow Fenton Street south on to SH5 – the route to Taupo.

Taupo town is sited on the shores of Lake Taupo, New Zealand's largest lake. Located just 90km (56 miles) south of Rotorua along a picturesque route featuring the famous Huka Falls, Taupo is a worthwhile day excursion.

A Thermal Wonderland

About 20km (12½ miles) south of Rotorua on SH5 you will pass the turn-off to **Waimangu Volcanic Valley** (daily 8.30am– 5pm; admission fee; tel: 07 366 6137; www.waimangu.com), a hot-bed of thermal activity created during the 1886 eruption of Mount Tarawera. Attractions here include **Waimangu Cauldron** and the **Inferno Crater** and **Ruamoko's Throat**. An interesting walk through the valley, returning by shuttle bus, takes about 1–2 hours.

Back on to SH5 and further 10km (6 miles) south you will pass the **Wai-o-Tapu Thermal Wonderland** turn-off (daily 8.30am–5pm; admission fee; tel: 07 366 6333; www.geyserland.co.nz). Waiotapu is famous for the **Lady Knox Geyser** which blows its top at 10.15am each day – thanks to a little human help – and the boiling **Champagne Pool**, which flows over green silicate terraces.

SH5 joins with SH1 just 2km (1¼ miles) before Wairakei. Just past Wairakei, on your left, look for the turn-off to the **Volcanic Activity Centre** (daily 10am–4pm; admission fee; tel: 07 374 8370; www.volcanoes.co.nz) which has informative displays on the region's geography. Other interesting activities in the area are the world's only geothermal **Prawn Park** (daily 11am–4pm; admission fee; tel: 07 374 8474; www.prawnpark.com) and the **Honey Hive** (daily 11am–4pm; admission fee; tel: 07 374 8553; www.honey.co.nz) along Huka Loop Road.

Huka Falls and Taupo

Moving on, follow the signs from the car park for a thrilling adventure on the **Waikato River**, courtesy of **Huka Jet** boat rides (daily 10am–5pm; tel: 07 374 8572; www.hukajet.co.nz). The adrenaline-pumping ride is guaranteed to leave you breathless. If you want to watch some of the action before going on the ride, turn left out of the car park and follow the signs 2km (1¼ miles) to the Wairakei Park and the Huka Falls car park. A short walk takes you to views of the thundering **Huka Falls**, on the upper reaches of the Waikato River.

When your river adventure ends, leave the car park and follow the loop road again. You will pass the **Huka Village Estate Conference Centre** on your right, and come to a lookout on the left side of the road, where there are panoramic views of Lake Taupo.

Vast Lake Taupo may seem serene, but don't be fooled by its current guise – as a volcano it erupted 28 times in the past 27,000 years. The hot springs and spas in the area are testimony to the fact the lake hasn't run out of steam yet. Dropping down SH1 into Taupo, you will find the **Taupo Visitor Centre** (tel: 07 376 0027; www.laketauponz.com) to your right on **Tongariro Street**. Park by the lake-front and see what is on offer. Highly recommended is a cruise on the *Ernest Kemp*, a replica 1920s steamer (daily departures at 10.30am and 2pm; extra sailing at 5pm from Jan–Apr; tel: 07 378 3444). Cruises leave from the wharf at the western end of Lake Terrace. The lake is famous for its fishing, and if you have time, the Visitor Centre can match you up with an experienced skipper or guide.

For lunch try the **Replete Food Company** at 45 Heu Heu Street (tel: 07 378 0606) and if you are there for dinner, opt for the unique setting of **The Bach** (pronounce *batch*) at 116 Lake Terrace (tel: 07 378 7856).

If you have more time, a fun activity is a bungy jump over the Waikato River with **Taupo Bungy** (tel: 07 377 1135; www.taupobungy.co.nz). Just beyond the jump site is a park area with an easy walk from the lower carpark down to the river's edge. You can even paddle for free in a natural hot spring that mixes with the cold and clear river water.

Towards Wellington

Just 5km (3 miles) back up SH1, on the return trip to Rotorua, is the turn-off to the **Craters of the Moon** (daily 9am–5pm; free; tel: 07 378 9833), another eerie thermal landscape, steaming rather than exploding, with interesting walks. Retrace your route back to Rotorua, or stay the night in Taupo before continuing south to Wellington. The 380-km (236-mile) journey on SH1 takes 5 hours and goes past Turangi and then along the Desert Road to Waiouru, Taihape, Bulls, Levin and then down the Kapiti Coast to **Wellington**.

Left: frothy Champagne Pool, Wai-o-Tapu Thermal Wonderland
Above: Huka Falls in a rage

rotorua & environs

Wellington & Environs

8. WELLINGTON'S HIGHLIGHTS *(see map, p45)*

This walking tour takes you from Te Papa Tongarewa museum to Lambton Quay and then up by cable car for lunch with spectacular city views. Stroll to the Beehive and Parliament Buildings, then return to your starting point via Queen's Wharf and Frank Kitts Park.

The starting point of this itinerary is Te Papa Tongarewa, The Museum of New Zealand, at Cable Street. If the weather is not ideal for walking, opt for the City Circular bus which leaves outside the museum at 10-minute intervals.

Every week, thousands of people visit **Te Papa Tongarewa – Museum of New Zealand** (daily 10am–6pm, Thursday 10am–9pm, tel: 04 381 7000; www.tepapa.govt.nz) confirming it as the city's star attraction. The NZ$317 million museum is the capital's prime visitor attraction and well worth a close inspection. There are interactive displays, virtual reality games and special exhibitions. Activities change daily, so get a map from the helpful staff in the foyer. Check out the Maori myths and legends of creation, experience a simulated earthquake, see the bones of the giant moa, and take a walk outside over a swing-bridge and through a recreated section of native bush.

The City Centre

To see more of the city, head north out of Te Papa and follow the water's edge towards the city's commercial centre. Watch out for in-line skaters as you make your way past the rowing clubs by **Frank Kitts Park**. This will lead you to the city's impressive **Civic Square**, with the **Michael Fowler Centre** and the Edwardian **Town Hall** in one corner and the city library in another. In between is the **City Gallery** (daily 10am–5pm; free), known for its contemporary art exhibitions, and the well sign-posted **Wellington Visitor Information Centre** (daily 9am–6pm; tel: 04 802 4860; www.wellingtonnz.com).

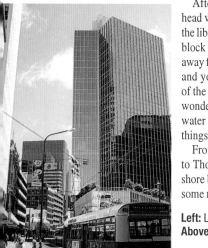

After picking up more information on the city, head west, leaving the square by the archway near the library. Cross Victoria Street and walk one more block to Willis Street. Turn right and then veer left away from the high-rise **State Insurance Building** and you are now on **Lambton Quay** – the heart of the city's commercial and retail area. If you are wondering what a quay is doing when there is no water in the immediate vicinity, the answer is that things were very different 150 years ago.

From **Wakefield Street**, along Lambton Quay to Thorndon Quay, marks Wellington's old foreshore before an earthquake in the 1850s reclaimed some more land. Explore the renovated **Old Bank**

Left: Lambton Quay
Above Right: Wellington Cable Car

Arcade diagonally opposite the State Insurance tower, with its boutique shopping and stunning design.

Lambton Quay is where commerce meets the commercial. Banks, accountancy and law firms occupy space here, and on **The Terrace** a block behind, while at ground level shop owners vie for some of the country's best and most expensive retail space. If you want to shop, then Lambton Quay is probably the place to do it.

Walk about 150m (164yds) along Lambton Quay looking for the sign for **Wellington Cable Car** (Mon–Fri 7am–10pm, Sat–Sun 9am–10pm). The cars leave every 10 minutes from Lambton Quay and take you effortlessly up a steep incline, under the motorway and over Kelburn Park to Upland Road and a magnificent view back over the city and its harbour. Have lunch at the **Skyline Café** (tel: 04 475 8727) overlooking the city and then, if the weather is good, take a stroll around the adjacent **Botanic Gardens** (open daily; free).

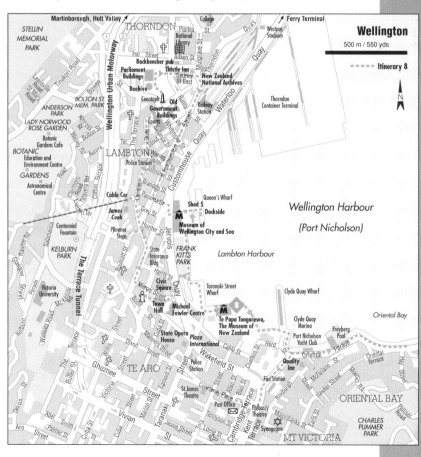

Wander off the main paths to fully appreciate the gardens, but ultimately aim for the **Education and Environment Centre** (Mon–Fri 9am–4pm, Sat–Sun 10am–4pm; free), where you learn about New Zealand's flora from a variety of interesting displays. Thereafter, return to the cable car for the trip back down to Lambton Quay. Turn left out of Cable Car Lane and enjoy browsing in the downtown shops. There are plenty of good options for some afternoon coffee along the way, including **Astoria**, on your right just past the renowned **Kirkcaldie and Stains Department Store**.

The Seat of Power

Cross over Bowen Street at the end of Lambton Quay and you are at the seat of political power in New Zealand. The circular, copper-domed building, known as the **Beehive**, houses the executive wing of Parliament, including the office of the Prime Minister. Walk past the **Cenotaph**, through the gates, and follow the sweeping drive up to the Beehive and the adjacent **Parliament Buildings**, built in 1922. Follow the signs out front to the tour desk for an informative guided tour (45-minute tours run hourly from Mon–Fri 10am–4pm, Sat 10am–3pm and Sun 12–3pm; free; tel: 04 471 9503).

The tour starts with a short video and then a guide will lead you through the halls of power. You will also be treated to a fascinating insight into how the building was 'earthquake-proofed' during recent renovations.

The **Old Government Building** is another place of interest, which you may have seen diagonally opposite the Cenotaph on your way to the Parliament Building. The grand Old Government

Building was completed in 1876 and constructed entirely of wood. The structure, using more than 9,290sq m (100,000sq ft) of timber, is claimed to be the largest wooden building in the southern hemisphere.

If you're thirsty, head 50m (55yds) up Molesworth Street, which runs in front of the parliament grounds, to the **Backbencher** pub and café (tel: 04 472 3065) at No. 34. It follows a political theme (including its menu) and is decorated with cartoons and caricatures of local political figures. I can guarantee you will see the Prime Minister here in some shape or form.

From the Backbencher, drop down East Sydney Street 50m (55yds) to Mulgrave Street. Turning right takes you to the **National Archives** (Mon–Fri 9am–5pm; Sat 9am–1pm; free; tel: 04 499 5595) to view items including the nation's founding document, the Treaty of Waitangi.

Queen's Wharf Area

From the National Archives, head down Mulgrave Street back to town. Passing the Railway Station on your left, head south down Featherston Street six blocks to the intersection with Panama Street. Turn left here and cross Customhouse Quay to return to the waterfront area. Explore the **Queen's**

Above: spot a politician or two at the Backbencher pub

Wharf waterfront and the **Events Centre**. Visit the **Museum of Wellington City and Sea** (daily 10am–5pm, free; tel: 04 472 8904; www.museumofwellington.co.nz), which is just next to the Customhouse Quay entrance to Queen's Wharf. The museum houses a captivating collection of maritime memorabilia. If you want to rest your feet, relax at the **Shed 5 Restaurant and Bar** (tel: 04 499 9069).

If, however, you are feeling energetic then **Ferg's Rock and Kayak** (Shed 6; tel: 04 499 8898; e-mail: wn@fergskayaks.co.nz; www.fergskayaks.co.nz) on the harbour side of the Events Centre complex can have you climbing walls or paddling on the harbour in minutes. The facility is owned by former Olympic kayak champion Ian Ferguson. Taking a kayak out for a paddle is great fun if the weather is good and in an hour you can easily cruise around past Te Papa to the fountain in Oriental Bay. If you don't want to get wet, then you could also try some in-line skating along the promenade or stick to walking back around the waterfront past Frank Kitts Park to Te Papa Tongarewa, The Museum of New Zealand.

Oriental Parade

If there is any time left in the day and the weather is shining you should carry on around the waterfront past the Overseas Ferry Terminal to **Oriental Parade**. Stroll around the boardwalk for great views back over the city, and of some of Wellington's prime real estate clinging precariously to the slopes of Mount Victoria.

Return via Courtney Place, Wellington's primary entertainment precinct. At the intersection with Kent Terrace is the grand old **Embassy Theatre**, venue of the world premiere of the final installment of *The Lord of the Rings* trilogy directed by New Zealander director Peter Jackson. Up Courtney Place, on your left, is where you will see **Westpac St James Theatre** (77–87 Courtney Place, tel: 04 802 6917; www.stjames.co.nz). This theatre plays host to many international musical acts. **The Jimmy Café and Bar** (Mon–Thur 7.30am–6pm, Fri 7.30am–9pm, Sat 9am–2pm), which is situated just inside the entrance of the theatre, is the perfect place at which to conclude your sightseeing for the day and to plan your evening's entertainment over a coffee.

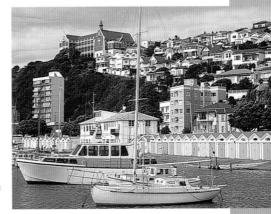

Above: bollards at Queen's Wharf
Right: Oriental Parade

9. MARTINBOROUGH *(see map below)*

This easy day driving itinerary takes you out of Wellington along SH2, over the Rimutaka Ranges and into the Wairarapa region. Highlights include views from the Rimutakas, the small and pretty town of Featherston, and the wineries of Martinborough.

Start this itinerary in front of the Railway Station on Bunny Street. Head towards the harbour and left on to Waterloo Quay. Drive past the Westpac Trust Stadium and follow the signs to the Wellington/Hutt motorway.

Martinborough is an 80-km (50-mile) drive from Wellington, but the drive can take longer than you expect because of the winding road over the Rimutaka Ranges and the volume of traffic on the motorway that links Wellington to Upper Hutt. To avoid the congestion of rush-hour, have a leisurely breakfast and head away after 9am.

This route takes you along the westerly edge of Wellington Harbour. There are several sets of traffic lights that slow your progress as you pass by Lower Hutt, Stokes Valley and then Upper Hutt. After Upper Hutt, SH2 begins its climb over the Rimutaka Ranges. Stop in the car park area of the café at the summit for views over the bush-clad hills to the **Wairarapa** region. Resuming your journey, a drive of a further 16km (10 miles) brings you to **Featherston**. Indulge in an ice cream cone at the Kia Ora (Maori for 'hello') Dairy on the left-hand side of the road

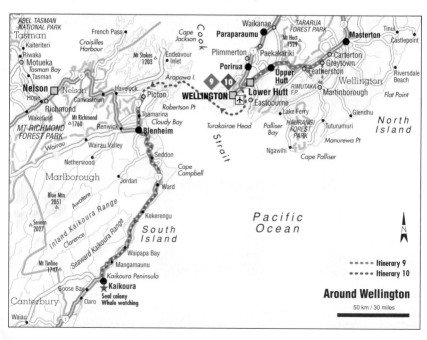

Around Wellington

50 km / 30 miles

just as you drive into town. You can pick up information on the region from the **Featherston Information Centre** on Fitzherbert Street (daily 10am–3pm; tel: 04 308 8051;www.wairarapanz.com), in the Old Courthouse building on the main street. On the corner of Fitzherbert Street and Lyon Street is the **Fell Engine Museum** (Sat–Sun and school holidays 10am–4pm; admission fee), which houses the only remaining Fell locomotive in the world.

After allowing about half-an-hour in Featherston, continue north along SH2. Just 1km (½ mile) out of town you will pass a **POW Memorial** site that has an interesting place in New Zealand's history. The memorial is on the site of a former WWI army training barracks, which was later used to hold Japanese soldiers captured in the Solomon Islands during WWII. During an attempted breakout from the camp in 1943, 48 Japanese POWs were killed.

Greytown and on to Martinborough

Continue the drive for another 15km (9 miles) north of Featherston to Greytown. **Greytown** is New Zealand's first planned inland town, and despite its name, it is anything but colourless. Its main street is lined with classic examples of wooden Victorian architecture. Spend some time browsing through the craft shops and learn more about the region's history with a visit to the **Cobblestones Museum** on 169 Main Street (daily 9am–4.30pm; admission fee; tel: 04 304 9687). Look out also for the huge eucalyptus tree as you drive down its main street. While it was being taken as a seedling from Wellington to Carterton by wheelbarrow, it was 'borrowed' en route by a local named Samuel Oates. It is hard to hide the stolen property now.

Allow an hour in Greytown before heading for your next destination: **Martinborough**. To get there, return back south down the main street and veer left off SH2 following the signs. Martinborough, a 15-km (9-mile) drive south-east of Greytown, is the centre of Wairarapa's burgeoning wine industry. You will pass several vineyards on the way into town, and the **Martinborough Information Centre** on 18 Kitchener Street (daily 10am–4pm; tel: 04 306 9043; www.wairarapanz.com) to get some advice about activities in town and wineries to visit.

Two of the more established vineyards are **Palliser Estate**, back down the main Martins Road (daily 10.30am–4.30pm and till 6pm on Sat and Sun in summer; tel: 04 306 9019; www.palliser.co.nz), and **Te Kairanga**, also on Martins Road (daily 10am–5pm, vineyard tours Sat and Sun at 2pm; tel: 04 306 9122; www.tkwine.co.nz). Palliser is a great place for lunch; alternatively try **Medici** on Kitchener Street near the town square. Take your time enjoying the relaxed country atmosphere. Drift back from your wine tastings around mid-afternoon and take a stroll around the craft shops. If you are enjoying your time in the country, stay a night at the elegant colonial-style **Martinborough Hotel** (tel: 04 306 9350; www.martinboroughhotel.co.nz).

The itinerary ends by returning along SH53 before taking the turn-off 6km (4 miles) out of town that cuts back through to Featherston. From there, you retrace your path back along SH2, over the Rimutakas to Wellington.

Above Left: switchbacks lead to Martinborough
Right: the expansive Palliser Estate

10. BY FERRY TO THE SOUTH ISLAND *(see map, p48)*

A full-day excursion by Interisland Line ferry through Cook Strait to Picton, then driving or joining a bus for a tour of the Blenheim wineries.

This could either be a day trip from Wellington and back, or a continuation of your journey to the South Island.

Using Wellington as a base, you can make a day trip to **Picton** in the South Island, visit the wineries of **Blenheim** and return to Wellington. **Interisland Line** offers such a trip in the summer (www.interislandline.co.nz; tel: 0800 802 802). Catch the *Lynx* ferry at the Waterloo Quay ferry terminal at 8am and arrive in Picton at about 10.15am after sailing across Cook Strait. From Picton, a bus will take you to the **Montana** winery, then to **Hunters** winery for lunch and on to the **Forest Estate** winery and distillery for more tastings. The bus returns you to the *Lynx*, suitably inebriated, for the 4pm sailing to Wellington, which should have you safely back in the capital around 6.15pm.

If You Drive

If you prefer to drive, the following itinerary gives you the flexibility of connecting to the South Island. Interisland Line runs scheduled ferry services between Wellington and Picton. If you've rented a car, take it on the ferry with you, or hire a car in Picton. The ferry crossing takes slightly over 2 hours on *The Lynx* catamaran and 3 hours on the *Aratere* or *Arahua* ferries. Visit the **Picton Information Centre** (tel: 03 520 3113; www.picton.co.nz) on the town's foreshore for maps and information, then journey on SH1 through to Blenheim.

At Blenheim, call in any one of a number of wineries that produce some of the country's best sauvignon blancs. Then, continue on SH1 to **Kaikoura** on the South Island's east coast. 'Kaikoura' means 'crayfish food', courtesy of the region's bountiful sea-life. Recommended is a tour with **Whale Watch Kaikoura** (tel: 03 319 6767; www.whalewatch.co.nz). Trips run four times daily and take you offshore to view some of the world's biggest mammals in their natural environment. You can also frolic with dolphins in the deep waters of the Pacific Ocean with **Dolphin Encounters** (tel: 03 319 6777; www.dolphin.co.nz). Note: drive time from Picton to Blenheim is 30 minutes; Blenheim to Kaikoura, 2 hours, and Kaikoura to Christchurch, 2½ hours.

Above: a dolphin encounter off Kaikoura

Christchurch & West Coast

11. CHRISTCHURCH'S HIGHLIGHTS *(see map, p52)*

Stroll along the banks of the Avon River and ride a tram to the Arts Centre and the Botanic Gardens. Take a boat ride on the Avon River, then return to the city centre for some shopping in Cashel Mall. Wind up the day with a ride up to Port Hills on the Mount Cavendish Gondola.

Begin this walking itinerary at the Christchurch Visitor Centre in Cathedral Square (Mon–Fri 8.30am–5pm, Sat–Sun 8.30am–4.30pm; tel: 03 379 9629; www.christchurchnz.net). Convenient parking is available at the public car park just next to Rydges Hotel.

Christchurch is an elegant city; English in style and grace, and nestling in the extinct volcanic landscape of the Port Hills. Sweeping away north, south and west are the expansive **Canterbury Plains**. East is the Pacific Ocean which has butted up grey-sand beaches and punctured the valleys of the **Banks Peninsula** to form numerous natural harbours.

Tram Tour

After checking out activities on offer at the Visitor Centre, venture out on to **Cathedral Square**. Buy a ticket for the historic **Tramway** that stops on Worcester Street (daily 9am–6pm and till 9pm in summer; tel: 03 366 7830; www.tram.co.nz). It is worth doing a full circuit on the tram just to get your bearings before disembarking and venturing out on foot. (If the weather is bad you can just hop on and off the tram on any of its stops.) The tram does a circuit via the Arts Centre, the Museum, Christ's College, Victoria Square, New Regent Street and back to Cathedral Square.

Do the complete circuit then disembark at Worcester Street Bridge. It is walking time. Head north along Oxford Terrace, past Rydges Hotel, following the river to Gloucester Street. Turn left and cross the Gloucester Street Bridge, and you will find a path that leads along the Avon River's west bank beside the **Canterbury Provincial Council Buildings** (guided tours from Mon–Sat 10.30am–2.30pm). The buildings are the only remaining provincial government buildings in New Zealand. A 100-m (109-yd) walk brings you out on to Armagh Street opposite the Law Courts, and if you cross back over the river you will arrive at **Victoria Square**.

Above: ride Christchurch's Tramway
Right: Provincial Council Buildings

Wander around the square – always alive with activity – at your leisure. Statues of Queen Victoria and Captain Cook grace the square in front of **Hamish Hay Bridge**, reputedly the first cast-iron and stone bridge of its type in New Zealand when it was built in 1863.

Beyond the bridge to the left of the amphitheatre is the **Floral Clock**, a feature of this 'Garden City' for many decades, while to the right of the Crowne Plaza Hotel is the **Christchurch Town Hall**. The **Victoria Street Café** on the entrance level of the Crowne Plaza Hotel (tel: 03 365 7799) is a perfect place for a meal. Or else, go next door to the café at the Town Hall and ask for a table overlooking the Avon River.

Along Avon River

Leave Victoria Square by crossing the north-south running Colombo Street and follow **Oxford Terrace** as it resumes winding its way along the banks of the **Avon River**. On your left you will see the beautifully restored **Retour Restaurant**, converted from a band rotunda, and the site of a punting operation on the river. Ahead, a strand of poplar trees line the Avon River, making for a particularly beautiful scene when draped in their autumn colours.

Turn right into Manchester Street and in the distance you should see the Port Hills. Turn right again into Armagh Street where the first left brings you to **New Regent Street** with its charming Edwardian façades painted in pastel blues and yellows. The street is closed to all vehicular traffic except the city's historic tram. Cafés now share the street with boutique shops.

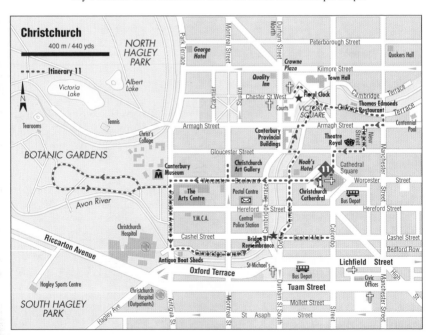

Cathedral Square

Turn right into Gloucester Street past the Theatre Royal and then first left into Colombo Street and you are at the geographic centre of Christchurch, **Cathedral Square**. The pedestrian-only area attracts a wide cross-section of Christchurch society. Like Victoria Square, it is a busy lunch-time venue and often features council-run activities in the summer. An interesting character you may see around (he 'disappears' from June to mid-August) is **The Wizard of Christchurch** (www.wizard.gen.nz) who takes to a soap-box at lunchtime in summer and holds forth on a variety of topics. Do not treat him lightly as he has been granted the status of 'A Living Work of Art'.

Prime position in the square is held by the grey-stoned **Christchurch Cathedral** (daily 8.30am–6pm), with its 63-m (208-ft) tower. Visitors can climb up to lookout balconies via a spiral staircase of 134 steps for panoramic views of the city. There are also free guided tours of the cathedral given at 11am and 2pm from Monday to Friday, 11am on Saturday and 11.30am on Sunday. Around the perimeter of Cathedral Square are a number of duty-free shopping and retail outlets and the offices of the South Island's largest daily newspaper, *The Press*.

Culture and the Arts

Leave Cathedral Square by heading past the statue of John Robert Godley, the city's founder, and west along Worcester Boulevard. Cross the Avon River, following the tram route for one block. At the corner with Montreal Street is the new **Christchurch Art Gallery** (daily 10am–5pm, till 9pm on Wed; tel: 03 941 7300; www.christchurchartgallery.org.nz). This is the largest public art gallery in the South Island and houses an impressive permanent collection of paintings, sculpture and ceramics as well as regular special exhibits.

When you're done, head another block west along Worcester Boulevard until you reach the **Arts Centre** (Information Centre open 9.30am–5pm; free tours 10am–3.30pm). The neo-Gothic stone buildings formerly housed Canterbury University, but now is a focal point for artists and craftspeople. Attractions here include the **Court Theatre**, the restored den of Nobel Prize winning physicist Sir Ernest Rutherford and the **Academy Cinema**. There are a wide variety of craft studios within the complex, so browse around. This whole area comes alive on weekends with a market from 10am–4pm. Sample some of the offerings from the exotic food stalls.

Located at the end of Worcester Boulevard, at Rolleston Avenue, is the **Canterbury Museum** (daily 9am–5pm; donation; tel: 03 366 5000; www.cantmus. govt.nz) which houses a variety of interesting displays, including the world-class Edgar Stead Hall of New Zealand Birds and the Hall of Antarctic Discovery. Free guided tours are conducted at 10.15am, 11.30am, 1.15pm and 2.30pm daily.

North of the museum are the grounds of the private boys' school, **Christ's College**, while south and west are the extensive grounds of the **Botanic**

Above Left: colourful New Regent Street facades
Right: the Gothic-inspired Christchurch Cathedral

Gardens (daily 7am till sunset; free). Established in 1863, the gardens are a remarkable transformation given the fact that the land was once covered in tussock and bracken. Take a leisurely stroll through the gardens to the tea kiosk. A battery-powered tour vehicle takes visitors on guided tours daily, leaving from outside the garden's Information Centre.

Leave the gardens and have lunch back at **Le Café** (tel: 03 366 7722) at the bottom end of Worcester Boulevard. Then head right on Rolleston Avenue to rejoin the Avon River by the Christchurch Hospital. If you are up to it, try a popular Christchurch family pastime – boating on the Avon – with paddle boats available for hire from the **Antigua Boat Sheds** (tel: 03 366 5885). Alternatively, buy an ice cream from the Boat Shed Snack Bar and continue along the river.

About 200m (218yds) across Montreal Street and around the river, the road joins Cashel Street. To your right is the distinctive archway of the **Bridge of Remembrance**, a World War I memorial. Cross the bridge and the road to **Cashel Mall**, another paved pedestrian-only area lined with shops. End this part of the tour by browsing along the mall or quenching your thirst at one of the numerous café/bars along Oxford Terrace.

Port Hills

To round off your day in Christchurch, take an afternoon excursion out of the city centre. Top of the list is a ride up Port Hills on the **Christchurch Gondola** (daily 10am till late; tel: 03 384 0700; www.gondola.co.nz). The gondola takes you on a 500-m (1,640-ft) vertical rise ride to the rim of the extinct Lyttelton volcano. From the viewing gallery, on a clear day, you get a spectacular view of Christchurch over to Lyttelton Harbour, out to the Pacific Ocean and over the Canterbury Plains to the Southern Alps. A restaurant and souvenir shops offer diversions after the ride up. The hardier can hire mountain bikes at the summit for an alternative route down. A free shuttle bus service, the Gondola Bus, leaves at regular intervals from the city centre.

Above: Arts Centre market
Left: punting on the Avon River

12. Akaroa *(see map, p56)*

A full-day driving itinerary around the base of the Banks Peninsula to the French-settled town of Akaroa. Walk the quaint streets and visit craft shops. Take a harbour cruise on the Canterbury Cat and have lunch at the French Farm Winery on the opposite shore before returning to Christchurch at mid-afternoon.

Start at Christchurch's Cathedral Square and head south along Colombo Street to Moorehouse Avenue. Turn right and travel to the end of the road where it joins up with the corner of Hagley Park. Follow the sign left into Lincoln Road, over the railway line and out along what becomes SH75.

Akaroa, just 84km (52 miles) from Christchurch, holds a unique place for many in the history of New Zealand. But aside from that, it is simply a wonderful place to visit, and easily reached by car from Christchurch.

Heading out of the city along SH75 you will pass through Halswell and Tai Tapu. South of Motukarara, the road will pass alongside Lake Ellesmere, a large coastal lagoon, before turning sharply left and following beside the picturesque Lake Forsyth. Just beyond the head of the lake is the settlement of **Little River** where you can stop and look at the crafts on display in the old railway building.

Continuing on, the road climbs steeply out of Cooptown and up to the appropriately named **Hilltop Tavern**. Drive in to the car park for a grand view over the **Onawe Peninsula** and **Akaroa Harbour**. The peninsula was the site of a Maori *pa* (fortified village), constructed in 1831 by the Ngai Tahu people to meet a threat of invasion from a northern Maori tribe. Drive down past Barry's Bay, Duvauchelle and Takamatua and finally to **Akaroa**.

Akaroa's Highlights

The town has a fascinating history, evidenced by the French-language road signs as you drive in. In 1838, Jean Langlois, the captain of a French whaling ship, negotiated the purchase of Banks Peninsula from a local Maori chief. On his return to France he organised a group of emigrants who sailed for Akaroa. They arrived in the Bay of Islands only to hear that the Treaty of Waitangi had been signed and British sovereignty over New Zealand declared. The emigrants decided to continue on to Akaroa and settle anyway. In 1849, Langlois' settlement company sold its assets and land claims to the New Zealand Company. In 1850, the French settlers were joined by a larger group of British colonists.

The French influence has remained strong and can best be experienced by walking around the charming streets at the northern end of the town. Find a parking space just as you enter Akaroa and walk along **Rue Lavaud**. Visit **Langlois-Eteveneaux Cottage** and the

Right: the route to Akaroa

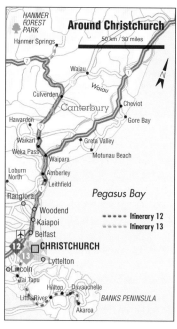

Akaroa Museum (daily 10.30am–4pm; admission fee; tel: 03 304 7614) on the corner of Rue Lavaud and Rue Balgueri. The cottage, prefabricated in France, is one of the oldest in Canterbury. Behind the cottage, the museum has interesting displays.

Also on Rue Balgueri is **St Patrick's Church**, built in 1863. Walk up Rue Balgueri to **Settlers Hill** and a track takes you to **L'Aube Hill Reserve** and the **Old French Cemetery**, the first consecrated burial ground in Canterbury. Walk back to Rue Lavaud and enjoy a stroll south beside the gardens, with its centrepiece **War Memorial**, to the sweeping beachside promenade. On a nice day you can easily walk the mile around the bay to the English part of town, taking in the views across the inlet. Otherwise, drive the same route and look for a car park near the Akaroa pier, a popular place for fishing.

Cruise and Lunch

Sign up for a cruise on the **Canterbury Cat** that plies the harbour at 11am and 1.30pm (tel: 03 304 7641; www.blackcat.co.nz). On the 2-hour trip to the headlands, you can visit a salmon farm and look for one of the world's smallest and rarest dolphins, Hectors Dolphin, and perhaps the world's smallest penguin, the White Flippered Blue Penguin.

If you return hungry, there are many eating places along Beach Road, like **Bully Hayes** at No 57 (tel: 03 304 7533). If it is summer and you want a treat, circle back around the harbour, carry on past Barry's Bay and along the low road to the **French Farm Winery** (tel: 03 304 5784; www.french farm.co.nz). Lunch casually alfresco on wood-fired pizza or indulge in the French provincial cuisine inside. Return via the Hilltop Tavern to Christchurch.

13. HANMER SPRINGS *(see map, p56)*

This full-day itinerary takes you north of Christchurch through rich farmland of the Canterbury Plains to the hot springs resort of Hanmer. See bungy jumpers hurl themselves off Thrillseekers' Canyon, climb Conical Hill, walk the forests and have a refreshing soak in the thermal pools before embarking on the return journey to Christchurch.

Drive out of the city along Victoria Street, heading away from the Crowne Plaza Hotel and continuing across Bealey Avenue along Papanui Road and, ultimately, on to the motorway and SH1.

Hanmer Springs, 135km (84 miles) from Christchurch, with the drive taking about 2 hours, is nestled amongst the foothills of the Southern Alps. It is also the South Island's main thermal resort. Surrounded by vast tracts of indigenous and native forests in a landscape cut by sometimes meandering and at other times roaring rivers, a day trip to Hanmer Springs combines scenic beauty with plenty to do.

Along the route you will cross wide shingle river-beds that drain from the Southern Alps. About 10km (6 miles) beyond Amberley, start watching for signs to some of the region's top-class wineries. A recommended option to break your journey is to visit the **Canterbury House Winery** at 780 Glasnevin Road (daily 10am–5pm; www.canterburyhouse.com; tel: 03 314 6900) 8km (5 miles) north of Amberley or **Waipara Springs Winery** (daily 11am–5pm; tel: 03 314 6777; www.waiparasprings.co.nz) just 4km (2½ miles) north beyond the Waipara Bridge. This vineyard offers great food in a courtyard setting to complement their wines.

To continue on your way, return to Waipara Junction, just beyond the Waipara Bridge. The turn-off to SH7 (sign-posted to Lewis Pass) signals the half-way point in your itinerary. If you skipped the wineries you can have tea or coffee at the **Waipara Tea Junction** (tel: 03 314 6769).

Driving on you will come to the birch-lined **Weka Pass** (named after a cheeky native New Zealand bird). Between Waikari and Culverden is the historic **Hurunui Hotel** (tel: 03 314 4207), with its peaceful garden bar and traditional pub atmosphere. The Hurunui holds the longest continuous licence of any pub in the South Island, having been in operation since 1860.

Thrills and Spills

About 126km (78 miles) from Christchurch is the SH7A Hanmer turn-off. Make the turn, but watch for the car park 200m (219yds) ahead on your right. Turn into the car park for dramatic views of **Thrillseekers' Canyon**. A short walk to the Waiau Ferry Bridge will show you how the gorge got its name. Bungyjumpers leap from the bridge and into the fast-flowing Waiau River, where spectacular jet-boat rides and rafting trips are offered too. Enjoy the view or join in the activities, then continue on to Hanmer, about another 8km (5 miles) up the road.

The very helpful **Hurunui Visitor Information Centre** at Amuri Avenue (daily 10am–5pm; tel: 03 315 7128; www.hurunui.com), run by the Hurunui District Council, is

Left: sheep rule the roads in New Zealand
Right: signage at Thrillseekers' Canyon

adjacent to the hot pools, on the left as you enter the town. It can provide you with lots of information, including accommodation options and details of some wonderful bush walks in the area.

One walk you must do is up the zig-zag track on **Conical Hill**, just behind the town. To get to the start of the track, walk directly on past the main shops and up Conical Hill Road. The track leads away from the top of the road and the walk can easily be done in half-an-hour. The lookout at the top offers magnificent views over the Hanmer Basin.

For lunch, try the **Alpine Village Inn** at Jacks Pass Road (tel: 03 315 7005) just behind the shopping centre, home-cooked café food at the friendly **Village Plus Café** (tel: 03 315 7124) on Conical Hill Road, or try one of the many cafés in the village.

Hanmer's Thermal Springs

The thermal springs of Hanmer were discovered by ancient Maori who used to rest here on their travels to collect greenstone from the West Coast. A European settler stumbled upon the springs in 1859; 20 years later, the government took control of the springs, using its curative waters to help rehabilitate wounded soldiers and the psychologically disturbed. The **Hanmer Springs Thermal Reserve** at Amuri Avenue (daily 10am–9pm; admission fee; tel: 03 315 7511; www.hotfun.co.nz) is now the central attraction of the town.

After relaxing you can retrace your way back to Christchurch, perhaps renewing your acquaintance with the Hurunui Hotel pub. It is generally filled with local farmers or raucous skiers in the evening, depending on the time of year. Either way, it is a nice way to round off your day.

Alternatively, you could dine at the well regarded **Old Post Office Restaurant** at Jacks Pass Road (dinner only; tel: 03 315 7461), stay the night at

the **Alpine Lodge Motel** at 1 Harrogate Street, opposite the thermal pools (tel: 03 315 7311; www.alpinelodgemotel.co.nz), and then continue your journey the next day westwards by following SH7 over the Lewis Pass to link with the West Coast itinerary on the following pages.

Above: bungy jump if you dare
Left: Hanmer Springs
Right: the Southern Alps

14. THE WEST COAST *(see pull-out map)*

A 3-day drive itinerary that offers an alternative route to Queens-town. It takes you from Christchurch's Pacific coast to the Tasman Sea via the Southern Alps, and then down through some breathtaking scenery to Franz Josef and Fox glaciers. From there, you follow Haast Pass through to Wanaka and on to the next hub, Queenstown.

Using Christchurch's Canterbury Museum on Rolleston Terrace as a starting point, head north, keeping Hagley Park on your left. Turn first left along Harper Terrace and follow the small blue aeroplane signs that direct you right onto Fendalton Road towards the airport. Fendalton Road leads to Memorial Avenue and some 3km (2 miles) down the avenue is a roundabout at the junction with Russley Road. Turn left and follow the signs to SH73 towards Arthur's Pass.

The 260-km (161½-mile) route over the scenic **Arthur's Pass** to Hokitika on the West Coast is one of great geographical contrasts. Initially you head out across the expanse of the Canterbury Plains on a route parallel to the Waimakariri River and also the main train line to the West Coast. The route takes you through Darfield, and then from Sheffield to **Springfield**, 70km (43½ miles) from Christchurch. SH73 climbs swiftly beyond Springfield into the foothills of the Southern Alps. At the same time, the scenery becomes much more dramatic.

Follow the road over **Porter's Pass** (923m/3028ft), which passes Lake Lindon and the turn-off to Porter's Pass skifield, before you pass **Kura Tawhiti** (Castle Hill Reserve). **Cave Stream Scenic Reserve** is 6km (4 miles) further. Look for the car park which has good views of the basin area, and, if you have an hour to spare and aren't afraid of enclosed spaces, explore the 362-m (1,188-ft) limestone cave through which the stream flows. Cave art inscribed on the walls indicate that Maori once inhabited this place. You will need warm clothes, torches with spare batteries – and a change of clothes when you exit the cave.

Arthur's Pass

SH73 passes lakes Pearson, Grassmere and Sarah before rejoining the Waimakariri River. About 40km (25 miles) beyond Castle Hill is the historic **Bealey Hotel**; another 10km (6 miles) and you are at **Arthur's Pass Village** – nestled in a bush-covered river valley among the mountains and the gateway to **Arthur's Pass National Park**. There is a **Department of Conservation Visitor Centre** on the left heading into the village (daily 8am–5pm; tel: 03 318 9211) with displays on local flora and fauna, and a short video clip recalling the story of how the first pass crossing was made. There is also information on a wide variety of walks in the area. If there is time, take the 2-km (1¼-mile) track known as **Devil's Punch Bowl** which takes you to the base of a 131-m (430-ft) waterfall.

There is a café just beyond the Visitor Centre but **The Chalet**, on the right of the main road at the west end of the village, is the best place for lunch. If you want to enjoy more of the alpine scenery The Chalet is also a good place to stay (tel: 03 318 9236; www.arthurspass.co.nz).

Heading on from the village the road climbs steeply for 4km (2½ miles) to the pass itself (912m/2992ft)and then descends steeply via the recently constructed (and quite spectacular) **Otira Viaduct**. Carry on past the old railway township of **Otira**. You are now on the West Coast – also known as the Wild West Coast or the Wet Coast.

Maori came here for *pounamu* (greenstone), then European settlers for gold. It is rugged countryside and a good way to experience it is the Shantytown experience. To get there, follow SH73 through the town of **Kumara** and then on to Kumara Junction. At the junction head north on SH6, and

follow the signs to Greymouth, but 8km (5 miles) before the West Coast's largest town you will see the Shantytown turn-off on your right. **Shantytown** (daily 8.30am–5pm; admission fee; www.shantytown.co.nz) is a mix of replica and restored buildings. Though authenticity is not its strong point, the gold-mining theme town can be fun. You can ride on a steam train and try your hand at gold panning.

Hokitika

Instead of spending the night at Greymouth, I recommend backtracking on SH6 and continuing 40km (25 miles) south to the town of **Hokitika**. The distances to other attractions further south make Hokitika a perfect nightstop. Try the **Jade Court Motor Lodge** at 85 Fitzherbert Street (tel: 0800 755 885; www.jadecourt.co.nz) or the stylish bed and breakfast **Villa Polenza** at Brickfield Road (tel: 03 755 7801; www.villapolenza.co.nz) with its views of the sunset from outdoor bathtubs.

Hokitika boasts some of the best restaurants on the coast. Try **Café de Paris** at 19 Tancred Street (tel: 03 755 8933), which has a Mediterranean theme and also does good breakfasts. There isn't much to do in the evenings except perhaps catch a movie at the Regent cinema (15 Weld Street) or the free glow-worm dell a kilometre north of the centre of town beside SH6.

The next morning visit the **West Coast Historical Museum** (daily 9.30am–5pm; admission fee), accessed via the **Hokitika Visitor Centre** at the corner of Tancred Street and Hamilton Street. After the museum visit, pick up the Hokitika Heritage Trail leaflet from the Visitor Centre and take a brief walk around town.

To the Glaciers

There is a lot of driving to do today so don't linger. Fill up with petrol, make sure you've got some cash on hand (because there are no banks until you get to Wanaka or Queenstown) and head back out on SH6. The glaciers are 148km (92 miles) south. On the way you will pass through the town of **Ross**, where the largest gold nugget in New Zealand, the 3.1kg (7 lbs) 'Honourable Roddy', was found. The Visitor Centre at 4 Aylmer Street (daily 9am–4.30pm; admission fee) has some information about the area.

Drive another 25km (15½ miles) further south and watch out for the giant sandfly that marks the small settlement of **Pukekura**. Stop at the **Bushman's Museum and Bushman's Centre** (daily 9am–5pm) for an entertaining insight into West Coast life.

Carry on another 4km (2½ miles) past the beautiful Lake Ianthe. SH6 takes you on through Harihari and then **Whataroa**, renowned as the breeding grounds for the graceful *kotuku* or white heron. Access to the heron's breeding grounds is restricted to only tours run by **White Heron Sanctuary Tours** (tel: 03 753 4120; www.whiteherontours. co.nz). Next on the coast is **Okarito**, famous for its lagoon. The area is also the retreat of Booker prize-winning writer Keri Hume. With the glaciers looming ahead, however, you should keep moving on.

Above Left: soaking in the sun
Left: road to Arthur's Pass. **Right:** weathering the cold

Franz Josef and Fox

Your first stop in **Franz Josef Glacier** – the village –should be the **Visitor Centre** (daily 8.30am–5pm; tel: 03 752 0796) for maps and information on things to do in the area. For half- and full-day guided tours of Franz Josef Glacier, contact **Franz Josef Glacier Guides** (tel: 03 752 0763; www.franzjosefglacier.co.nz). There are also scenic plane rides and helicopter flights to either Franz Josef and Fox glaciers and/or **Mount Cook** *(see below)*.

Alternatively, if you prefer to tackle the glacier on your own, drive over the Waiho River and turn right for a further 5-km (3-mile) to the glacier. A 90-minute walk along a 4-km (2½-mile) trail from the carpark will take you face to face with this giant river of ice. However, without the right kind of shoes, you won't be able to get onto the icebed.

The best accommodations are found in Franz Josef village if you decide to stay the night. The **Franz Josef Glacier Hotel** (tel: 03 752 0729; www.scenic-circle.co.nz) is nice and homey. Dinner at the **Beeches Restaurant** (tel: 03 752 0721) along the village main road is a perfect way to end the night.

Fox Glacier, 25km (15½ miles) further south, is a smaller village than Franz Josef. To get to the glacier itself, drive through the town and turn left on to Glacier Road. You'll reach a carpark after 6km (4 miles) and from there it is a 30-minute walk to the face of the glacier. If you prefer a guided tour, make inquiries at its **Visitor Centre** (daily 8.30am–5pm; tel: 03 751 0807) or book direct with **Alpine Guides** (tel: 03 751 0825; www.foxguides.co.nz).

From Fox Glacier, head back out to the main road and on to SH6. There is a lot of distance to cover from here. Driving via the **Haast** pass, it's 267km (166 miles) to **Wanaka** and 338 km (210 miles) to **Queenstown**.

15. MOUNT COOK *(see pull-out map)*

A 2-day drive itinerary from Christchurch via Mount Cook to Queenstown. Spend the night in Mount Cook, take a scenic flight to the glaciers of the Southern Alps and continue to your next hub, Queenstown.

If you don't have time to drive, but would still like to see the glaciers and peaks of the Southern Alps and Mount Cook, the direct Air New Zealand flight from Christchurch to Queenstown offers spectacular views along the way.

Above: walking on ice
Right: Mount Cook is New Zealand's tallest peak

From Christchurch to Queenstown via Mt Cook

The drive from Christchurch to Mount Cook covers a distance of 331km (206 miles) and will take about 5 hours. From Mount Cook it is a further 262km (163 miles) to Queenstown, another 4 hours on the road. This is a long but very scenic drive so it's certainly worth considering.

From Christchurch, take the SH1 southwest across the fertile Canterbury Plains. Take the turn-off into SH79 some 50km (31 miles) past Ashburton and drive past Geraldine and Fairlie before joining with SH8 and the journey over **Burke Pass** to **Lake Tekapo**. The serene **Church of the Good Shepherd** overlooking the lake is a favourite photo spot. Stop by the lake for a stretch and a snack before continuing on. Make another stop at **Lake Pukaki** to enjoy the dramatic views of Mount Cook and then take the turn-off into SH80 for the 55-km (34-mile) drive along the western shore of the lake to **Mount Cook Village**. Depending on what time you arrive, make bookings ahead for a thrilling skiplane flight with Mount Cook Ski Planes *(see below)* to the glaciers and Mount Cook either on the same day or the next.

The most comfortable accommodations at Mount Cook Village is **The Hermitage** (tel: 03 435 1809; www.mount-cook.com). Surrounded by majestic mountains, the hotel – with a range of hotel and chalet rooms – is an ideal but pricey stopover destination to break up the long drive.

Mount Cook is New Zealand's highest mountain at 3,764m (12,348ft). From its small airport on SH80 you can take a **Mount Cook Ski Planes** flight (tel: 03 435 1026; www.skiplanes.co.nz) to view some awe-inspiring scenery. The **Glacier Highlights** tour covers the length of the **Tasman Glacier** and makes you feel as if the ice is close enough to touch. The magnificent stillness and quiet of this landscape has to be experienced to be appreciated.

The magnificent **Grand Circle** option lasts for about an hour and flies you to the **West Coast** of the main divide. You will first view, and then land on either the **Franz Josef Glacier** or **Fox Glacier** *(see page 62)* and then step out on to these spectacular ice floes. There is the thrill of the take-off on ice, and more stunning scenery as you cross the divide again and swoop over the **Tasman Glacier**, the longest temperate glacier in the world.

There are various walks as well as heli-skiiing in the area if you want to linger for another few days. If not head for Queenstown by returning to SH80 and continuing south on SH8 past Twizel and Tarras. Past Lowburn, take the turn-off right into SH6 and continue into **Queenstown**.

christchurch & west coast

Queenstown
& Environs

16. QUEENSTOWN'S HIGHLIGHTS *(see map, p66)*

Ride the Skyline Gondola for a panoramic view of Lake Wakatipu and Queenstown. Head down and walk along the waterfront, perhaps signing up for a jet-boat ride on the Shotover or Kawarau rivers. Have lunch and then join the TSS *Earnslaw* on an afternoon excursion to Walter Peak, capping the day off with a stroll around Queenstown Gardens.

Start your day at the Queenstown Visitor Centre in the Clocktower Building on the corner of Shotover Street and Camp Street (daily 7am–6pm; tel: 03 442 4100; www.queenstown-vacation.com). Pick up some maps and get advice on the huge range of outdoor activities on offer.

Resting on the shore of Lake Wakatipu, with high peaked mountains looming all around and valleys cut deep by swift-flowing rivers, **Queenstown**, in central Otago, is the quintessential year-round holiday resort. The town mixes the charm of its history and the grandeur of its natural setting with a dash of brashness that accompanies most resorts of its kind. The result is that, day or night, there is always something to do there.

Skyline Gondola

Have a strong cuppa at **The Naff Caff** at 66 Shotover Street (tel: 03 442 8211) and begin your itinerary by crossing Shotover Street and walking two blocks north-west up Camp Street. Turn left into Isle Street, past the fire station and then first right into Brecon Street to the **Skyline Gondola** (daily from 10am till late; tel: 03 441 0101; www.skyline.co.nz). The gondola rises 450m (490yds) up Bob's Peak to a magnificent view of Queenstown, **Lake Wakatipu** and **The Remarkables** mountain range. A walking track at the top takes you to what has become a New Zealand icon – a bungy jump. This particular operation called **The Ledge**, run by bungy pioneer A J Hackett (tel: 03 442 7100; www.ajhackett.com) offers spectacular views of Queenstown (if you manage to keep your eyes open!) as you take the plunge.

There is also a **Skyline Restaurant**, a gift shop and an outdoor viewing deck. Speed demons can take the chairlifts to a higher elevation and take the exciting luge, or three-wheel cart ride, down while the more sedate can sign up for *Kiwi Magic* – a 30-minute movie showcasing the scenic splendour of New Zealand (daily 11am–9pm).

Coming down from the Gondola on Brecon Street, you will find another activity that may

Left: Lake Wakatipu boatman. **Above Right:** Skyline Gondola. **Right:** jet-boating on Shotover River

tempt you: **Caddyshack City** (tel: 03 442 6642), an elaborate mini-golf centre. Otherwise, wander down Brecon Street, turn right at Shotover Street and follow the road around to the **Steamer Wharf Village** where there are shops and restaurants. The wharf is also home to a variety of vessels, but none so distinctive as the TSS *Earnslaw*, which was launched in 1912 and affectionately known to locals as 'The Lady of the Lake'. The coal-fired boilers belch out the *Earnslaw*'s trademark black smoke as she carries passengers on sightseeing tours. Book your cruise tickets with **Real Journeys** (six cruises daily in summer; tel: 03 442 7500; www.realjourneys.co.nz) for the 2pm excursion to **Walter Peak**.

Shotover Jet-boat Ride

Now it is time for some action in the form of a thrilling jet-boat ride. **Shotover Jets** (tel: 03 442 8570; www.shotoverjet.co.nz) operate on the famous **Shotover River** 6km (4 miles) from town. A courtesy bus departs from the station opposite the Queenstown Visitor Centre on Shotover Street, taking the adventurous out to the jetty near **Arthur's Point** at regular intervals. The jet-boat drivers are top-class and their sense of humour can be gauged by the smiles on their faces as they take you to within inches of overhanging rocks! Depending on time, you may want to lunch at **Cavell's Restaurant**

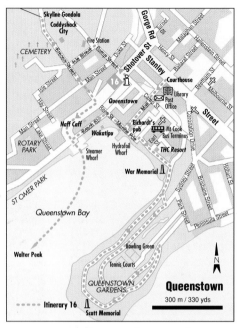

Itinerary 16 ⚓
Scott Memorial

Skyline Gondola
Caddyshack City
Fire Station
CEMETERY
Gorge Rd
Shotover St
Stanley
Queenstown
Courthouse
Library
Post Office
Naff Caff
Wakatipu
Eichardt's pub
Mt Cook Bus Terminus
ROTARY PARK
Steamer Wharf
Hydrofoil Wharf
THC Resort
War Memorial ⚓
ST OMER PARK
Queenstown Bay
Walter Peak
Bowling Green
Tennis Courts
QUEENSTOWN GARDENS
Queenstown
300 m / 330 yds
N

(tel: 03 442 6550) at Arthur's Point which overlooks the jet-boating antics from a spectacular perch. Although the boat ride only takes 30 minutes, add another hour for the ride to the river and back.

On your return you may feel like getting your 'land-legs' back by wandering around the **waterfront** and **The Mall** area. Though much of Queenstown has been taken over by modern tourist development, its charm is maintained by some of the century-old buildings, including the renovated **Eichardts'** pub – in operation since 1871, now a lodge and stylish bar – on Marine Parade and the courthouse and library buildings at the corner of Ballarat Street and Stanley Street, built in the year 1876.

Cruise on the Earnslaw

If you haven't had lunch, head for **Vudu** (tel: 03 442 5357) at 23 Beach Street. As 2pm draws near, make your way back to the wharf for your 3-hour cruise on the TSS *Earnslaw* to **Walter Peak**. Situated on the western shore of the lake, Walter Peak is the original homestead of one of New Zealand's most famous sheep and cattle stations. The cruise across takes about 40 minutes and you have plenty of time to enjoy the beautiful gardens which surround the homestead. You also get to watch a sheep-shearing demonstration and inspect the rather unique herd of Scottish Highland cattle.

Return to Queenstown and round the day off with a late afternoon stroll around **Queenstown Gardens** on the other side of **Queenstown Bay**. Walk around past the jetty and along Marine Parade to the War Memorial.

Follow the tree-lined promenade just behind the beach front and take the path at the end into the gardens. Wander at your leisure around the gardens at the lower end of the peninsula, watching for the dramatic memorial to Antarctic explorer Robert Falcon Scott.

Circling back on the east side are views first over the Frankton Arm to Kelvin Heights, then out over the middle reach of Lake Wakatipu towards Walter Peak. Finally, return along the beach front to town.

Right: relaxing on the TSS *Earnslaw*

17. ARROWTOWN *(see map, p68)*

A half-day driving itinerary past the Shotover Gorge, Arthur's Point and up to Coronet Peak for a panoramic view of the Wakatipu Basin. Ascend and head for Arrowtown, visiting its old miners' huts. Return via Lake Hayes and the Kawarau Bridge bungy jump operation.

To get to Arrowtown from Queenstown, turn left off the north end of Shotover Street into Gorge Road. If you didn't do the jet-boat ride on Shotover River the day before (see page 65), this is your last chance.

A trip to **Arrowtown**, 21km (13 miles) from Queenstown, is a journey into the past. Nestled in a quiet gully, the town played a prominent role in the gold rush days of the 1860s. Arrowtown thrived as it drew in fortune seekers from around the world – an oriental flavour was added to the mix courtesy of hundreds of Chinese miners who joined the search for the increasingly elusive golden nuggets. As the gold diminished, so did Arrowtown's importance. It did not, however, go the way of desolation like so many other gold mining settlements in the vicinity. Instead, it just slipped back into a quieter style of life, revelling in its beautiful location.

The Shotover River

The route to Arrowtown is quite spectacular, lined with poplar trees that are stunning during autumn. About 6km (4 miles) out of Queenstown is **Arthur's Point Pub** (tel: 03 442 8007), worth an excursion on its own for its traditional pub food, beer and atmosphere. Some 500m (547yds) further is the historic **Edith Cavell Bridge**, spanning the scenic Shotover River.

Turn left at the end of the bridge and into the entrance to the **Shotover Jet-Boat** operation *(see page 65)*. If you haven't had the thrill of jet-boating, then perhaps you may be tempted now. If not, at least watch the boats and hear

Above: Lake Wakatipu with The Remarkables mountain range

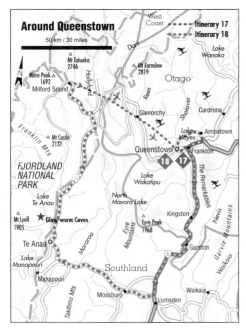

Around Queenstown

50 km / 30 miles

Itinerary 17
Itinerary 18

the screams as travellers are whisked under the bridge and through the spectacular Shotover Gorge. A good spot to watch from is **Cavell's Restaurant**, where you can contemplate the challenge over coffee, or something stronger.

Top Ski Fields

Continue along what is now Malaghan Road; passing Arthur's Point Camp Ground on your right and the **Shotover Stables** (tel: 03 442 7486) offering horse treks, on your left. Slow down as you pass **Nugget Point** (tel: 03 442 7273; www.nuggetpoint.co.nz), the luxury lodge overlooking the Shotover River, because just beyond is the turn-off left to **Coronet Peak** and **Skippers Canyon**.

While Skippers Canyon is off-limits to most rental cars, Coronet Peak is not. In winter, Coronet Peak is a top-class ski-field with a fully sealed access road, but at all other times of the year, it is a superb lookout point to view the Wakatipu Basin. The drive up to the peak and back is about 20km (12½ miles).

Every year, in early July, Coronet Peak comes alive as the focus of the Queenstown Winter Festival. Celebrity skiers, sheep dog trials, night skiing and all-night partying signal the start of the ski season in the region. You can look out from Coronet Peak over the Wakatipu Basin to **The Remarkables**, a dramatic mountain range that drops down to Lake Wakatipu and hosts another ski-field for more advanced skiers.

Arrowtown

Return to Malaghan Road, turn left and resume your journey to Arrowtown. If you are interested in art, make a stop along Dalefield Road about 1km (½ mile) past the Coronet Peak turn-off, where you will find several galleries.

As you drive on, watch out for the **Millbrook Resort** (tel: 03 441 7000; www.millbrook.co.nz), a high-class development combining resort-style accommodation and an 18-hole golf course designed by one of New Zealand's greatest golfers, left-hander Bob Charles. Just beyond Millbrook, turn left

down Berkshire Street and you are in **Arrowtown**.

Park your car and stroll down **Buckingham Street**, Arrowtown's main road. It feels like the set of some Hollywood movie, only a lot more authentic. There are craft and souvenir shops to browse around and also a number of historic landmarks – testimony to the small town's rich history. On the left, you will pass a monument to the Chinese goldminers who played an important role in the development of the region.

For shopping, try the **Arrow Emporium** (9–23 Buckingham Street). If you are after gold souvenirs, try **The Gold Shop** which sells crafted jewellery as well as nuggets at good prices. Just beyond The Gold Shop at **Athenaeum Hall** is a map and information board about Arrowtown, recounting some of the region's history, but for a more 'hands on' historical experience, go to the **Lakes District Centennial Museum** (daily 9am–3pm) just before the corner with Wiltshire Street.

After your history lesson, cross the road to **Crossroads** (tel: 03 442 1860) for a heart-warming New Zealand country-style lunch in a historic stone house over a century old. Just across the road from the Stone Cottage, in The Avenue of Old English Trees (the willow and sycamore-lined end of Buckingham Street), is Arrowtown's library, and behind that, further back is the old schist-built **Masonic Lodge**.

Panning for Gold

If you are feeling lucky, a great way to spend a half hour or so is to hire a gold pan from the friendly staff at **Hamilton's Grocery Store** back at the west end of Buckingham Street and try your hand at panning. Just go down to the river beyond the picnic area a block north of the main road and you meet the **Arrow River**. There is a fair chance you will garner a gold flake or two for your troubles.

To get a further insight into the hardships of mining a century ago, drive or walk to the **Arrowtown Chinese Camp**, 100m (109yds) west of the Marshall car park just as you entered the town. Walk between the plum and berry trees to the huts built into the hillside. Look for **Ah-Lum's Store** on the left at the start of the

Left: an autumn horse ride. **Above:** Arrowtown architecture
Right: Arrowtown once thrived on gold nuggets

small track and you might laugh at the Historic Places classification given to what looks like an old toilet. Note the lack of a door, and be amazed at the great views over Arrowtown from the facility.

There are several routes out of Arrowtown, but I suggest driving back along Berkshire, and instead of turning into Malaghan Road, continue on for a scenic drive past **Lake Hayes**. Turn left at the bottom of Lake Hayes, following SH6 about 10km (6 miles) until you reach **Kawarau Bridge**, site of another A J Hackett's bungy-jumping operation (www.ajhackett.com; tel: 03 442 7100). Join in if you dare, but it is equally fascinating to watch others take the 43-m (47-yd) plunge off the historic bridge with just a glorified rubber band to halt their fall. This site is one of the first commercial bungy jump operations in the world, fanning the craze that has swept the globe today. Return to Queenstown back along SH6.

18. MILFORD SOUND *(see map, p68)*

A day trip by coach to the spectacular natural glory of Milford Sound in Fiordland National Park. Cruise on the fiord and return by coach via the Homer Tunnel and Te Anau to Queenstown. Alternatively, take a scenic flight from Milford back to Queenstown.

The road trip is a tiring 4–5 hours each way so leave the driving to someone else. The Discover Milford Sound coach and boat excursion from Great Sights company is ideal. Book with The Station Information Centre (tel: 03 442 5252; www.thestation.co.nz). The coach departs from The Station at 7.30am from the corner of Camp Street and Shotover Street. Alternatively, enquire about a pick up from your hotel. Note: the return flight option is dependent on weather.

Milford Sound is an unspoilt wonderland in the rainforest area of New Zealand's deep south. Formed from a sunken glacial valley, Milford Sound

(actually a fiord) is surrounded by steep bush-clad cliffs rising to the rugged mountains of the Southern Alps. It is the spectacular final destination of the world famous Milford Track, but you can reach it easily from Queenstown in a day.

The 291-km (181-mile) road trip to Milford Sound takes you along one of the world's most beautiful scenic routes. The coach will take you along the edge of Lake Wakatipu beneath the rugged Remarkables mountain range, to **Te Anau** then on through the **Fiordland National Park** and the 1km long (½ mile) Homer Tunnel – with its rock walls dangerously close to the edge of the bus – before descending to the stunning Milford Sound.

Red Boat Cruise

Once there you will join the spectacular **Red Boat** cruise on the fiord. Ensure you bring your camera for some magnificent photo opportunities. You will see cascading waterfalls (successfully fill a cup of water from beneath **Fairy Falls** and you might earn a dram of whisky from the Red Boat captain!), the fabulous form of **Mitre Peak** (1,692m/5,551ft) rising almost vertically from the sea floor, rare southern fur seals and possibly cruise alongside dolphins. If you are there around Christmas-time, watch out also for the beautiful flowering southern rata, also known as the South Island Christmas Tree. On the side of some of the sheer cliffs you will see veins of green, indicating traces of mineral deposits in the mountains. The Maori discovered this and were early visitors to the fiords in search of sacred greenstone.

Depending on time, a recommended treat is the **Underwater Observatory** – a viewing chamber 12-m (40-ft) beneath the water line – so you can view life under the water as well as above it.

Bring a waterproof jacket with you because Fiordland boasts the highest rainfall levels in the country. It seldom dampens the experience, but sandflies can. They thrive in the dampness of the region and though not harmful, their bites are extremely annoying. Covering up and dousing yourself liberally with insect repellent helps.

The return coach trip will have you back in Queenstown by 8pm. A great option (and which saves time) is the exciting return trip by air (the bus driver will have more details). The flight passes over magnificent mountain peaks on the way back to Queenstown, so have your cameras ready.

Left: Milford Sound is ringed with mountain peaks
Above: Fairy Falls. **Right:** seals are aplenty at Milford Sound

queenstown & environs

Leisure
Activities

SHOPPING

For some people, shopping is the whole purpose of travel, while for others it is a necessary evil. No matter where you fit in the spectrum, shopping in New Zealand can be both enjoyable and enlightening. It can provide the impetus for getting out and about and mixing with the locals, as well an introduction to aspects of Kiwi history and culture. *(See page 92 for general retail hours.)*

Of the five centres that feature in the itineraries, the main cities of Auckland, Wellington and Christchurch offer the most diversity. International clothing labels vie with local names of style and quality such as Karen Walker, Zambesi and World. Budget-priced chains around the country include Glassons and Katies for women, and Hallensteins for men.

The main cities and the resort towns of Rotorua and Queenstown are also well stocked with stores selling traditional crafts and souvenir products. Queenstown is especially good for outdoor and adventure gear.

Woollens

New Zealand is one of the world's major wool producers, and experienced manufacturers take the raw material right through to quality finished products. Handknitted, chunky sweaters from naturally-dyed wool or mohair are ideal if you are heading back to a northern winter. Innovative wall hangings created from home-spun yarns make another worthwhile purchase.

Leather

The same farming heritage has led New Zealand to develop an extensive leather industry fed by skins from local tanneries that are amongst the world's best. Soft polished lamb suede is turned by craftsmen into superb designer dresses and jackets. Other excellent products include wallets, bags, leather jackets and gloves.

Sheepskin

With over 45 million sheep, it is little wonder that sheepskin is a major shopping attraction. Full-fleece sheepskin rugs in their natural state or processed are innovatively used for car-seat covers, floor rugs, mattress covers and baby rugs. Don't forget to buy warm, fleece-lined 'Ugg' boots.

Woodwork

New Zealand is blessed with unique and beautiful timbers, including the native kauri and rimu. Craftspeople are skilled at turning these timbers into works of art. Bowls and trays, or purely decorative polished wood pieces make ideal gifts.

Maori Carvings

The time-honoured skills involved in Maori carvings have been passed down from one generation to the other. Carvings usually tell stories from mythology and often represent a special relationship with the spirits of the land. Maori carvings of both wood and bone can command high prices, but cheaper options are available in the form of small pendants, often worn around the neck by both men and women.

Greenstone

Highly prized for traditional and spiritual reasons, greenstone (New Zealand jade) was formerly used by the Maori in ornaments and weapons. It is now used in jewellery and decorative items such as the Maori *tiki*

Left: food complements the great outdoors
Right: bowls made from kauri wood

(a pendant worn to bring good fortune). You can watch the stone being worked and also pick up some good bargains at greenstone factories in Auckland and on the West Coast of the South Island. The unique and beautiful final product is also widely available in shops all over the country.

Paua Shell
The paua fish (abalone) has been revered by Maori for centuries, not just for its flesh but for its delicate shell. The shell with its opalescent colours is polished and used for a variety of jewellery, trinkets and other small ornaments.

Pottery
Pottery is regarded as one of the most developed of New Zealand art forms and local potters are renowned for producing some of the finest ceramic art in the world. Examples of their work can be seen at many crafts shops. While driving, watch out also for roadside signs pointing to a potter's house. It is always a diversion worth taking.

Food
Savour the taste of New Zealand back home with its natural produce. Processed items like local jams, chutney, pates, smoked beef and honey do not need documentation, and make excellent gifts as they are attractively packaged. Indulge yourself with fresh local fruit like strawberries, kiwifruit, tamarillos or stone-fruit.

Wines
Wines are a real New Zealand success story. The country's young wines, with their fresh and exciting flavours, are jumping up and demanding attention in the international market. White varietal wines such as Sauvignon Blanc and Chardonnay are consistently well grown in New Zealand. Call in at local wineries or talk to people in bottle-stores or restaurants. They will be happy to guide you in the right direction if you wish to pick up a bottle or two.

Sports and Outdoor Equipment
New Zealanders love the great outdoors so it should come as little surprise that they have developed a wide range of hard-wearing clothing and equipment to match tough environmental demands.

Warm and rugged farm-wear like Swanndri bush shirts and jackets are popular purchases, while mountaineering equipment, camping gear and backpacks set world standards. Some items have even become fashion success stories, like the Canterbury range of rugby and yachting jerseys.

Auckland
New Zealand's largest city not surprisingly offers some of the country's most varied shopping. **Queen Street** is the obvious place to to find souvenirs, some of them quite classy. At the harbour end, downtown Queen Street hosts the major duty-free stores. For a full range of items, try the **DFS Galleria** on the corner of Customs Street and Albert Street.

Vulcan Lane, off Queen Street, will lead you to **High Street** and the **Chancery district**, where Auckland's major designer fashion boutiques are clustered.

For a completely different shopping experience, go to the **Victoria Park Market** (www.victoria-park-market.co.nz) at Victoria Street West. The market offers a huge variety of goods from leatherware to pottery.

Like the rest of the world, Auckland has plenty of suburban shopping options; most notable is **Newmarket**, which offers a great selection of shops, from well-known New

Right: a proud potter

Zealand chain stores to international designer stores.

Rotorua

General shopping is concentrated along the city's main road, **Tutanekai Street**, though there are also souvenir shops aplenty on **Fenton Street** near the Visitor Centre. Maori culture is to the fore in Rotorua and it is a good place to look for Maori arts and craft items, as well as leather and sheepskin products. **The Best of Maori Tourism** (corner of Fenton Street and Haupapa Street) offers original Maori-designed clothing and carvings in bone and wood. You can watch craftspeople at work at **The Jade Factory** at 1288 Fenton Street.

Wellington

The capital city has some capital shopping, centred on **Lambton Quay**. There is plenty of variety, ranging from main street chain stores such as **Farmers**, to clothing chain stores like **Country Road** and **Max**. **Whitcoulls** and **Dymocks** are two bookstores along the Quay for you to find your holiday reading.

Worth a special visit is the **Kirkaldie and Staines** department store at 165–177 Lambton Quay, a Wellington institution renowned for its quality products and old-fashioned good service.

Duty-free shopping is limited in Wellington though you can try **Duty-Free Stores** at the airport or Mercer Street in the city.

For crafts and antiques, you can spend a good hour or two browsing among the converted villas of **Tinakori Road**. If you are of a more alternative bent, the small designer clothing stores that compete for space with second-hand bookshops along **Cuba Street** will offer you plenty of ideas.

Christchurch

The **Arts Centre** on Worcester Boulevard is a great place to shop for a variety of handcrafted gift ideas. Antiques and prints are available from a wide variety of stall holders, while permanent shops within the complex include a gallery and carving studio.

Cashel Mall is the best bet for inner-city shopping. The pedestrian-only mall hosts boutique New Zealand fashion stores such as **Flame**, **Workshop** and **Plume** along with

international names such as **Esprit**. Christchurch's best known department store, **Ballantynes**, is on the corner of Cashel Mall and Colombo Street. Christchurch is well stocked with duty-free shopping on the north side of Cathedral Square. **DFS** and **Regency Duty-Free** both have outlets at the airport, where clothing, gift and bookshops cater for last-minute shoppers.

Queenstown

When it comes to tourists, Queenstown aims to please in just about every way. Souvenir shops are open daily with extended hours so you can buy just about anything, and at any time.

Jewellery, duty-free and craft shops fill **The Mall**, selling greenstone and bone carvings, handknitted woollens, and local honeys and jam.

O'Connells Shopping Centre hosts 25 stores under one roof at the corner of Camp Street and Beach Street. Given Queenstown's focus on outdoor activities, high-quality sportswear and sporting equipment is sold widely in the town. New Zealand's largest **Canterbury of New Zealand** store is located in O'Connell's Shopping Centre and sells a wide range of its famous All Blacks rugby-inspired clothing.

Steamer Wharf Village on the lake-front (Beach Street) has created a unique atmosphere with vibrant new shops and restaurants in a renovated building next to where the TSS *Earnslaw* docks.

Right: sample our seafood

EATING OUT

Dining can be a real pleasure in New Zealand, courtesy of the country's developing multicultural mix (European, Pacific and Asian) and its natural resources (fertile farmland and extensive coastline).

Although European influences are dominant, chefs have increasingly been turning to Asia and the Pacific for inspiration to expand their menus. There has been a surge in the number of ethnic Thai, Malaysian, Indian and Japanese eateries of world standards opening all over the country.

Another trend is towards a lighter and healthier style of cooking. And most restaurants have vegetarian dishes on their menus. The focus, however, always remains on fresh New Zealand produce.

Fish is abundant and of very good quality. Varieties include delicious freshwater salmon, sole and flounder. Whitebait – tiny minnow-like fish – is a seasonal delicacy.

Look for roadside stalls selling succulent crayfish, or splash out and try one if you find it on any menu. Green-lipped mussels are a popular item. In the summer you will find them tossed on barbeques and cooked in a tangy sauce as they are steamed open. Oyster varieties include the Pacific oyster, the rock oyster and the famed Bluff or Stewart Island oyster.

Meat, of course, is writ large on most menus in New Zealand. Lamb and mutton are often found traditionally roasted and served with a dollop of mint sauce. Beef comes in a variety of cuts but steaks like T-bone are found on most menus.

Vegetables are widely grown all around the country, and varieties you may be offered include aubergine (eggplant), silver beet (Swiss chard), asparagus and beans. The New Zealand pumpkin is tops as is the local *kumara* (sweet potato).

New Zealand wines, especially its white varietals, are often of very fine quality and compliment most cuisines favourably.

Fruit like kiwifruit, strawberries, raspberries, boysenberries and rock and watermelons are the mainstay of dessert menus, supplemented with rich ice creams. When driving, look for fruit stands, which in the north sell tropical and citrus fruits and apples, and in the south, apples and stone-fruit.

Recommendations

Tea rooms abound in New Zealand, serving light lunches of generally fried food, and snacks of pies, sandwiches and rolls washed down with weak tea and coffee. Major cities tend towards café and brasserie-type establishments – upping the octane rating of the coffee, throwing away the deepfryer, stylising the food and adding the designer touch to decor. Like everything, you get what you pay for. Restaurants open around 6pm and last orders can be had around 10pm. Note that BYO (Bring Your Own) indicates a restaurant licensed for the consumption and not the sale of alcohol. A three-course meal without drinks for one person is categorised as follows:

$ = NZ$40 and below
$$ = NZ$40–NZ$60
$$$ = NZ$60 and above

Above: a haven for meat eaters
Right: seafood galore

Auckland

Dining out is more a part of Auckland life than any other New Zealand city and there are plenty of options to choose from. All the main hotels have top-class restaurants and there are a plethora of cafés and casual dining options. **Ponsonby**, a short taxi ride west of the central city, is a trendy dining strip. The downtown **waterfront** area has several eateries with great views of the harbour, and **Parnell**, to the east, has some more established restaurants without the brashness of Ponsonby.

Euro
Princes Wharf
Tel: 09 309 9866
Fashionable restaurant that was *the* place to be during the America's Cup yachting regatta. The high-quality food and service continues with the focus on fresh New Zealand produce. $$$

The Observatory
Sky Tower
Tel: 09 363 6000
www.skycityauckland.co.nz
Venture nearly 200m (660ft) up Auckland's tallest structure to the highest restaurant in the tower for buffet-style New Zealand seafood specialities. $$–$$$

SPQR
150 Ponsonby Road
Tel: 09 360 1170
One of Auckland's most famous and best-loved restaurants, with great cuisine, notably the linguini and clams. It becomes a popular nightspot once the plates are cleared away. $$$

Wildfire
Princes Wharf
Tel: 09 353 7595
Meat and seafood abound in this Mediterranean eatery by the waterfront. Try the tapas menu, or something more substantial such as a gourmet pizza or something from the wood-fired grill. $$

Rotorua

Maori culture is to the fore here, and a *hangi* (traditional Maori cooking method where food is cooked underground for several hours) should be tried. *Hangi* is offered along with a Maori cultural show at several of Rotorua's main hotels. If you would like to have more international fare, most restaurants can be found around Tutanekai Street towards the lake.

Bistro 1284
1284 Eruera Street
Tel: 07 346 1284
Multi-award winning fine dining restaurant, situated in a historic building; strong emphasis on quality New Zealand produce. A good choice for a special occasion. $$$

Fat Dog Café Bar
1161 Arawa Street
Tel: 07 347 7586
Makes this list courtesy of its delicious and reasonably-priced breakfasts, lunches and coffees. Colourful and popular, this café is a good place to start the day, or to sit later on when you are writing those postcards home. $

Poppy's Villa
4 Marguerita Street
Tel: 07 347 1700
Great hospitality in this elegant Edwardian villa. Has won numerous awards for its beef and lamb dishes. Relaxed atmosphere and quality New Zealand meat and seafood. End your meal with the rich New Zealand ice cream dessert. $$

Right: striking a pose

Wellington

The capital draws many people in to serve the needs of government – and that seems to include many fine chefs. Asian and Indian influences are strong and the city boasts some of the best variety of restaurants in the country. Cuba Street has many cafés and inexpensive Malaysian and Thai restaurants. The lower end of Courtenay Place, towards Mount Victoria, is the best area to go for just about anything else.

Citron
270 Willis Street
Tel: 04 801 6263
Thirty-seater fine-dining restaurant with fare by award-winning chef Rex Morgan. Highly rated by food critics. Choice of a three-course menu or a superb degustation menu. $$$

The Flying Burrito Brothers
176–182 Cuba Street
Tel: 04 385 8811
Fun Mexican-styled eatery and bar in the Bohemian Cuba quarter. $

Logan Brown
192 Cuba Street
Tel: 04 801 5114
First-class location in an old bank building. Superb dining and a menu combining innovation with the best of New Zealand produce. An extensive wine list and top service mean this restaurant should be marked down for any special occasion. $$$

Shed 5
Queens Wharf
Tel: 04 499 9069
Great setting in a renovated harbour building, matched by good service and quality European (with inspiration from the Pacific) menu. Also sports a lively bar. $$$

Christchurch

Christchurch restaurants are going from strength to strength in both style and content. The city has broken out of its conservative shackles and this is reflected strongly in the vibrant cafés and restaurants along Oxford Terrace and Cashel Mall.

The Blue Note
20 New Regent Street
Tel: 03 379 9674
Offers great food with a Mediterranean influence washed down by live jazz. The ambience is warm and welcoming, the setting on the pedestrian-only New Regent Street is superb. $$

The Dux de Lux
41 Hereford Street
Tel: 03 366 6919
Laid-back dining in a restaurant/bar complex that overflows with activity. The menu is extensive and includes a large number of seafood and vegetarian options. Try a brewed-on-the-premises beer – Dux lager and Nor'wester ale are favourites – while you are there. The outdoor garden bar is a treat, winter or summer – and especially when there is a live band in attendance. $$

Honeypot Café
114 Lichfield Street
Tel: 03 366 5853
Casual eatery serving full meals as well as a selection of delicious sandwiches and pizzas with innovative toppings like tandoori chicken and cajun and sour cream sauce. Great desserts and coffee too, all at prices that won't break your wallet. $

Il Felice
56 Lichfield Street
Tel: 03 366 7535

Above: fine wines and fine food

A very popular Italian BYO restaurant. The owners, Paulette and Felice, pride themselves in recreating the full Italian experience, from fresh pasta right down to the passionate ambience. You are in for a special treat if Luciano is waiting tables when you dine. **$$**

Tiffany's Restaurant
Corner of Oxford Terrace and Lichfield Street
Tel: 03 379 1350
Fine wines and the best of regional cuisine. Tiffany's has a picturesque riverside location but is still close to the centre of town. Service is top class. Their al fresco lunches are also recommended. **$$**

Queenstown

Everywhere you look in Queenstown there is either a souvenir shop or a restaurant in view. The town caters for tourists in great style, and with a range of eating options you would normally only expect in a much larger place. Walk down The Mall and you will be absolutely spoiled for choice.

The Bathhouse
Marine Parade
Tel: 03 442 5625
www.bathhouse.co.nz
Located in an authentic Victorian bathhouse with scenic views of the waterfront. The romantic old-world ambience belies the innovative fusion cuisine served. Crab cakes with anise plum sauce and the duck poached in five spices are winners. **$$$**

The Birches
Nugget Point Resort
Tel: 03 442 7273
Located at the luxury Nugget Point Resort

10 minutes away from downtown Queenstown, the restaurant is well worth this minor inconvenience. Chef Randall Wadman turns the freshest of NZ produce into creative and innovative dishes. The herb-crusted rack of lamb is to die for. **$$$**

Boardwalk Seafood Restaurant & Bar
Steamer Wharf Village
Tel: 03 442 5630
Popular with tourists – in fact Bill Clinton dined here as well– it serves both meat and seafood dishes with sufficient flair. The service can be a little indifferent. **$$$**

Roaring Megs Restaurant
57 Shotover Street
Tel: 03 442 9676
E-mail: roaringmegs@xtra.co.nz
Fine dining in an original goldminer's cottage dating from the late 1800s. Flambé cooking is a speciality. This restaurant has won awards for its European/Pacific Rim style of cuisine. Candle-lit dining in a cosy and relaxed atmosphere. **$$**

Solera Vino
25 Beach Street
Tel: 03 442 6082
Intimate restaurant with a Mediterranean ambience. Start with tapas and then move on to the well presented mains. A good range of wines is also available. **$$**

Tatler
5 The Mall
Tel: 03 442 8372
With magnificent views of the lake, this restaurant offers table d'hote as well as a la carte dining, featuring game, seafood and regional specialties – in a gold-rush era building. **$$$**

Left: foil-baked salmon
Above: al fresco at Dux de Lux

Wellington's Michael Fowler Centre and St James Theatre, and the Christchurch Town Hall or Westpac Centre. A biennial highlight is the New Zealand Festival of the Arts in Wellington.

Throughout the summer, city councils in the major cities all hold themed events that boost activity levels even higher. Huge outdoor Christmas parties are held, Auckland has its Big Day Out music festival, Wellington its Fringe Festival, and Christchurch its Summertimes and Festival of Romance. Many activities surrounding these events are free and held at outdoor venues such as parks and domains. To keep up with these events check out the entertainment pages of the local daily newspaper or ask for details at the nearest Visitor Centre.

Sporting events provide another evening activity. Arenas such as Jade Stadium in Christchurch, Eden Park in Auckland, and Wellington's Westpac Stadium are the venues for night rugby in the winter, and test or day/night cricket matches in the summer. If matches are on, you can be sure it will be busy in the bars later that night – especially if the home team wins.

NIGHTLIFE

New Zealand's nightlife options can vary considerably, depending on the size of the place you are visiting. In small towns do not be surprised to find little more than a humble pub. Pubs are a great New Zealand social institution: enter one and you will seldom find yourself short of conversation or an opinion. In recent years, many city pubs have become more sophisticated, with 'boutique' beer brewed on the premises, brasserie-style food and more fashionable furnishings.

The main cities have a variety of cosmopolitan dance clubs with a predominantly young clientele, as well as late night bars for incurable insomniacs.

In Auckland and Wellington, and to a growing extent Christchurch, activity in the bars doesn't peak until after midnight. Auckland and Wellington are busy most nights of the week, while it is a little quieter in Christchurch until Thursday, Friday and Saturday nights. Queenstown reaches a critical mass at times, such as during the winter festival, when the parties don't seem to stop.

Drama, dance and classical music performances take place in all the larger cities, with international acts usually held at the town hall or major convention venues such as Auckland's Aotea Centre,

Auckland
Pubs/Bars
Loaded Hog
204 Quay Street
Tel: 09 366 6491
Big, brash and busy. Draws a young and happening crowd. Several bars and dancing till late; located down by the waterfront.

SPQR
150 Ponsonby Road
Tel: 09 360 1710
Ponsonby comes alive at night with its bars and clubs. At SPQR you can eat (Italian), and drink among the city's 'glitterati'.

Clubs
Coast
Level 7, Hewlett Packard Building, Princess Wharf
Tel: 09 300 9966
This is a large club, divided into different areas. Very popular at weekends with a mixed but stylish crowd.

Above: an Auckland dance club

Spy Bar
204 Quay Street
Tel: 09 377 7811
Sophisticated but the heavy dance music is no quieter for that. Definitely a see and be seen venue. Open till very late.

Casino
SKYCITY
Corner of Victoria and Federal streets
Tel: 09 363 6000
www.skycityauckland.co.nz
More than a thousand slot machines and a hundred gaming tables seek to lure the weak of spirit, as well as bars and restaurants.

Live Theatre
Maidment Theatre
8 Alfred Street
University of Auckland campus
Tel: 09 308 2383
www.maidment.auckland.ac.nz
Top quality professional theatre.

Classical Music
Aotea Centre
Aotea Square
Tel: 09 309 2677
www.the-edge.co.nz
Apart from classical music, this performing arts centre also features drama and dance performances. Check website for details.

Rotorua
Pubs/Bars
Barbarella
1263 Pukuatua Street
Tel: 07 347 6776
This is Rotorua's main live-music venue and you're as likely to find the latest punk band from Auckland as a DJ keeping things happening. Underground dance nights have incurred noise complaints.

Fuze Bar
1122 Tutanekai Street
Tel: 07 349 6306
This upmarket café and bar is the place to go for light gourmet meals and great coffee. In the evenings, it becomes one of the most popular bars in town with dance music.

Kaspers
1302 Tutanekai Street
Tel: 07 347 1144
An English-style bar, as its name suggests, with a good selection of beers and wines from all over the world.

O'Malleys Irish Bar
1287 Eruera Street
Tel: 07 347 6410
Open seven days, 11am until late. Nice atmosphere, friendly people and good music. Live entertainment every Friday night with happy hours from 5pm–7pm.

Pig and Whistle
Corner of Haupapa and Tutanekai streets
Tel: 07 347 3025
Features naturally brewed beers, a garden bar and live entertainment.

Wild Willy's
1240 Fenton Street
Tel: 07 348 7774
Café/bar with a distinctly Western theme and food. Live entertainment on Friday and Saturday nights.

Wellington
Pubs/Bars
Bouquet Garni
100 Willis Street
Tel: 04 499 1095
Perfect for a glass of wine in what are now plush surroundings. The stunning wooden building used to be a brothel; now it is upmarket and all class.

The Brewery Bar and Restaurant
Corner of Taranaki and Cable streets
Tel: 04 381 2282
This place has a viewing platform above the bar, which allows customers to watch their favourite beers being brewed. The bar also boasts the largest mural in Australasia.

Above: Aotea Centre at night

Dockside
Shed 3 Queens Wharf, Customhouse Quay
Tel: 04 49999
Also a club and a restaurant, Dockside rocks with a suited city crowd, particularly on Thursday and Friday nights. The setting is great and the dance floor can be crowded.

Hummingbird
22 Courtenay Place
Tel: 04 801 6336
A stylish place in a great location that attracts a more mature crowd than some of the other establishments along Courtenay Place. Try the tapas menu or a drink at the bar while you people watch.

Clubs
Studio Nine
9 Edward Street
Tel: 04 384 9976
A rave-style dance club that features guest DJ's playing the latest house and drum and bass music. Also sometimes a venue for over-seas acts. Filled to capacity on most nights.

Vurtigo
32 Courtenay Place
Tel: 04 382 8001
This is where the bartenders come for a drink, which helps explain why it's open from 3pm to 6am. Casual, with eclectic music and an intimidating line of ingenious cocktails.

Live Theatre
Bats Theatre
1 Kent Terrace
Tel: 04 802 4175
www.bats.co.nz
Cutting-edge theatre that features challenging performances in a small and intimate setting. Hosts fringe festival material yearly.

Downstage
Cambridge Terrace
Tel: 04 801 6946
www.downstage.co.nz
One of the reasons which make Wellington the country's theatre capital. Main venue for mainstream professional performances.

Classical Music
Wellington Festival & Convention Centre
(including Michael Fowler Centre)
Tel: 04 801 4231 for information
Also offers dance and drama performances.

Christchurch
Pubs/Bars
All Bar One
130 Oxford Terrace
Tel: 03 377 9898
One of several similar establishments along Oxford Terrace that are cafés by day and heaving bars by night. Start here and work your way along.

The Dux de Lux
41 Hereford Street
Tel: 03 366 6919
Trendy but laid-back crowd drink in either one of the two bars, or outside. Live music, often folk and blues. Brews its own beers.

The Loaded Hog
Corner of Cashel and Manchester streets
Tel: 03 366 6674
The premier bar on a busy corner. Like its Auckland counterpart it is big, bold and a popular place to be seen.

Clubs
Ministry Nightclub
90 Lichfield Street
Tel: 03 379 2910
Plays the latest sounds from around the world to a crowd often happy and often gay.

Above: Wellington takes pride as a city of the arts
Right: nightlife scene in Queenstown

Big dance floor and great sound system adds to the frenetic atmosphere late at night.

The Club
88 Armagh Street
Tel: 03 377 1007
Attracts an up-market clientele. Stricter dress code than most other clubs.

Live Theatre
Court Theatre
Arts Centre, 20 Worcester Street
Tel: 03 366 6992
A venue for professional productions.

Classical Music
Arts Centre
20 Worcester Street
Tel: 03 366 0989

The Town Hall
Kilmore Street
Tel: 03 366 8899
Home of Christchurch Symphony Orchestra.

Casino
Christchurch Casino
30 Victoria Street
Tel: 03 365 9999
www.christchurchcasino.com
Small but up-market casino. Gaming tables, slot machines, bars and top restaurants.

Queenstown
Pubs/Bars
Lone Star Café and Bar
14 Brecon Street

Tel: 03 442 9995
A busy Texas-style restaurant and bar that plays predominantly 60s and 70s music.

McNeill's Cottage Brewery
14 Church Street
Tel: 03 442 9688
Queenstown's only brewery, bar and restaurant. Its open fires and relaxed atmosphere are great in the winter, its garden bar equally welcoming in the summer.

Pog Mahone's
14 Rees Street
Tel: 03 442 5382
As Irish as they come in Queenstown. The Guinness flows smoothly and it packs out when live bands are playing – usually Wednesday and Sunday. Also functions as a restaurant.

Clubs
Surreal
7 Rees Street
Tel: 03 441 8492
It's a restaurant in the early evening but as the night goes on techno music takes hold and this venue transforms into one of the cooler nightspots in town.

The World
27 Shotover Street
Tel: 03 4426 757
Often filled with backpackers and young adventurers. This is a lively and often very noisy venue renowned for its very happy hours that go on till late.

CALENDAR OF EVENTS

The sunshine and longer days of summer from December through February mean that these months are always packed with regular scheduled events. The local councils of the major cities all organise a wide range of activities, including outdoor concerts and family picnic days. There are also many sporting events. For specific dates of events, please contact your nearest Tourist Information Centre *(see Practical Information pages 98–99)*. The following are a general listing of events.

December – February

New Year's Eve: 31 December. This signals the start of extended holidays for many families in New Zealand. Most cities have big public parties in their respective centres, with music and fireworks and much merry making at the midnight hour. Celebrations generally go well into the early hours of the new day.

Christchurch Floral Festival: January/February. This festival of flowers highlights the wonderful flora of Christchurch that give the city its other name, 'The Garden City'. Events include special flower shows and a Miss Floral competition.

Waitangi Day: 6 February. New Zealand's national day celebrating the signing of the Treaty of Waitangi. It is a public holiday, and in Waitangi itself (in the Bay of Islands, Northland), an official ceremony takes place at the Treaty House. The spectacular scene of Maori *waka* (war canoes) on the bay make it a special time to visit the Northland region

Auckland Anniversary Day Regatta: Last Monday of January. See why Auckland is called 'The City of Sails' when literally thousands of yachts of all shapes and sizes – from one person P-class yachts to majestic A-class keelers – take to the water at Waitemata Harbour for this annual event. The magnificent spectacle is best viewed from Mt Victoria on North Head or from ferry boats that cruise from the terminal in downtown Auckland.

Marlborough Wine and Food Festival: February. Special flights are arranged from Wellington and Christchurch to get people to this incredibly popular festival – celebrating the region's wonderful wine and creative cuisine – held in Marlborough at the top of South Island. The festival is usually a sell-out.

Super 12 Rugby: February–May. Perhaps the toughest rugby series in the world. Played

Above: Auckland Anniversary Day Regatta

between teams from New Zealand, Australia and South Africa at various venues in all three countries.

Pasifikal Arts Festival: Held every March in Auckland, this is a colourful series of cultural events performed by people from Polynesia, Melanesia and other Pacific islands, as well as crafts and food.

March – May

Ngaruawahia Maori Canoe Regatta: March. An annual event near Hamilton that sees the opening of the Turangawaewae Marae (Maori meeting house) to the public for the only time each year. The canoe regatta on the Waikato River is an important event in the Maori cultural calendar.

Golden Shears International Shearing Championships: March. Every year, Masterton (north of Wellington) hosts this unique event where the best of New Zealand sheep shearers gather to see who is the fastest bladesperson in the world.

New Zealand International Festival of the Arts: March. This biennial event is held in Wellington in even-numbered years, and attracts a wide range of world-class artists and musicians to the country for performances, exhibitions and demonstrations. Some events are booked up months in advance.

Around The Bays Fun Run: March. Tens of thousands of people turn out for this friendly run around Auckland's waterfront along a 11km (7 mile) route.

Royal Easter Show: March/April. This agricultural and farming showcase in Auckland is the largest of many held regularly around New Zealand at different times of the year. Farming equipment is displayed, and produce and animals are judged amidst a carnival atmosphere.

Arrowtown Autumn Festival: April. Arrowtown, near Queenstown in the South Island, holds a festival to honour autumn each year. There are all sorts of activities and parades but nothing is more spectacular than the glorious autumn colours.

June – August

Queenstown Winter Festival: July. Queenstown, in the central South Island, goes a little crazy every year with this festival of winter. *Aprés-ski* activities reach a peak at this time with parades and parties, while on the ski-slopes people dress up to get down. Because of the huge number of visitors Queenstown attracts at this time of the year, accommodation must be booked well ahead.

Ohakune Mardi Gras: August. Winter games in the Ruapehu and Turangi areas in central North Island.

September – November

Alexandra Blossom Festival: September/October. The blossoms in the stone-fruit growing area of Central Otago make spring a special time. It is celebrated in Alexandra, an hour by car from Queenstown, with a spectacular parade through town.

Kiwifruit Festival Week: September. This event in Te Puke, north of Rotorua, combines a variety of activities around a celebration of the furry fruit that is almost as much a symbol of New Zealand as the flightless bird it shares its name with – the kiwi.

Show Week: Mid-November. Held in Christchurch, this is one of the highlights of New Zealand's horse racing calendar. Both the New Zealand Trotting Cup and the New Zealand Galloping Cup are competed for within a space of days.

Guy Fawkes Night: 5 November. Fireworks and fun celebrating an obscure British antihero who attempted to blow up the Houses of Parliament in London.

Right: Carnival fun

Practical Information

GETTING THERE

By Air

New Zealand's relative distance from other population centres makes air travel the most common form of transport. New Zealand has two major international airports, with Auckland's (AKL) serving as the gateway to the North Island, and Christchurch's (CHC) serving as the gateway to the South Island. Wellington's airport (WLG), with its shorter runway, serves international flights only to and from Australia. All three airports have banking and exchange facilities covering the times of international flights. All have information desks for assistance, and major car rental firms have offices at all airport outlets.

New Zealand's national airline is **Air New Zealand** (www.airnz.co.nz). It operates an extensive service throughout the Pacific, linking New Zealand with Australia, Asia (including Japan), the Pacific Islands and the US. It also flies to and from Europe (London Gatwick and Frankfurt) via the US.

Other international airlines serving New Zealand include Qantas, British Airways, Singapore Airlines, Emirates, Korean Airlines, Air Pacific, Thai International, Canadian Airlines, Garuda Indonesian, Malaysian Airlines, Continental Airlines, Cathay Pacific, Japan Airlines, Polynesian Airlines, UTA and Aerolineas Argentinas.

From the Airport

Auckland Airport: Situated 22½ km (14 miles) south of the city centre. Travel time is between 40 minutes and one hour depending on traffic. A coach service runs to the city every 30 minutes on the hour and half-hour from 7am to 10pm. A taxi to the city is more expensive (NZ$40–50), or you could join others in a shuttle bus (around NZ$25). A bus links the international terminal with the domestic terminal, or alternatively you can take a trolley and walk the 900m (984yds).

Christchurch Airport: Located 11 km (7 miles) from the centre of the city. Travel time is about 30 minutes. There is a shuttle bus service (NZ$12) and taxis (NZ$20) are available. A coach runs every 30 minutes from outside the terminal to the city.

Wellington Airport: Situated 8 km (5 miles) from the centre of the city. Travel time is about 30 minutes. A coach service runs every 20 minutes, shuttle buses (NZ$12–15) service the major hotels, and taxis (NZ$22) are available outside the terminal building.

By Sea

No shipping companies currently operate scheduled passenger services to New Zealand on a regular basis. Some companies, however, include the country on itineraries of cruises in the South Pacific.

For further information, check with your travel agent, or shipping companies such as P&O Lines, Cunard, Royal Viking Line and Sitmar Lines.

TRAVEL ESSENTIALS

When to Visit

New Zealand has four distinct seasons and though temperatures are seldom extreme, visiting at different times of the year offers different experiences. Summer runs from December to February (Christmas in New Zealand is very often an outdoor event involving a barbecue); autumn from March to May; winter from June to August; and spring from September to November.

The most settled weather is usually between February and April. In winter, New Zealand's mountains come to the fore, with plenty of activities available for travellers interested in winter sports

Left: panoramic vistas

such as skiing. If you are a beach or water-sports person, then summer is definitely the time to visit. Springtime can be cool but with blossoms on the trees it is also a very pretty time of the year.

Visas and Passports

All visitors to New Zealand require passports which must be valid for at least three months beyond the date you intend leaving New Zealand.

Visa requirements differ, depending on nationality, purpose of visit and length of stay. Check with your nearest New Zealand diplomatic or consular office.

Entry Formalities

New Zealand has three levels of control at all points of entry into the country: immigration, customs and agriculture. Every person arriving in New Zealand must complete an arrival card which will be handed out on the aircraft. Travellers face a NZ$200 instant fine if they bring in foodstuffs, plants and plant or animal products without declaring them to agriculture officials for inspection.

Vaccinations

No vaccination certificates are needed for entry into New Zealand. However, if within three weeks of your arrival you develop any sickness such as a skin rash, fever and chills, diarrhoea or vomiting, you should consult a doctor and tell him you have recently arrived from overseas.

Customs

Goods brought into the country will not be subject to customs duty or sales tax provided they are for personal use and are taken out of the country on departure. Apart from personal effects, visitors are allowed the following concessions free of duty, provided they are over 17 years: Cigarettes, cigars, tobacco – 200 cigarettes or 50 cigars or 250g of tobacco, or a mixture of all three not weighing more than 250g; alcoholic liquor – 4½ litres of wine (equivalent to six 750ml bottles), and two 1,125ml bottles of spirit or liqueur. Goods up to a total combined value of NZ$700 are free of duty.

Weather

The climate ranges from sub-tropical in the north (in summer this can mean rain showers and humidity) to temperate in the south. Overall temperature variations are limited because of the proximity of most parts of the country to the moderating influence of the sea. However, the rugged countryside does tend to lead to wide local weather variations within relatively small areas. Inland areas such as the centre of the South Island can be hot and dry in the summer, and icy cold in the winter. Prevailing weather patterns from the west tend to be wetter than from the east, particularly in the South Island where the Southern Alps act as a 'rain shadow' for the eastern regions. Southerly winds bring in cool air, though this often means fine weather on the West Coast.

Clothing

New Zealanders tend to take life casually, and this is reflected in the clothes they wear. They tend to dress informally for most occasions. And in all but the best hotels and nightclubs, fashionably smart clothes (perhaps a jacket for men, trousers and shoes) are all that is necessary.

In late autumn, winter and early spring, you would need a warm all-season coat, and perhaps gloves and a hat if you are heading inland or to the mountains.

In late spring, summer and early autumn, garments of cotton and cool washable materials are recommended. Shorts and T-shirts are commonly worn but you should also

Above: seasons are reversed in the southern hemisphere, so pack the right clothes

pack a sweater and light jacket. A water-proof jacket is especially valuable in the wetter northern and western regions.

Electricity
Electricity is supplied domestically throughout New Zealand at 230 volts, 50 hertz AC. Most hotels and motels, however, provide 110-volt AC sockets for electric razors only.

Time Difference
New Zealand is 12 hours ahead of Greenwich Mean Time. Summer Time, where clocks are advanced one hour, operates from the last Sunday in October until the first Sunday in March. If you fly west to New Zealand you lose a day when you cross the International Date Line.

GETTING ACQUAINTED

Geography
New Zealand is situated in the South Pacific between latitudes 34° and 37° South. It is a long and narrow country, lying roughly north-south and comprising two main islands separated by the Cook Strait. It is bordered by the Pacific Ocean to the east and the Tasman Sea to the west. Mountain ranges run through much of New Zealand's length. The nearest major land mass to New Zealand is Australia, 1,930 km (1,200 miles) northwest.

New Zealand is slightly larger in size than the British Isles at 269,057 sq km (103,883 sq miles). Two-thirds of the country are mountainous and dissected by swift flowing rivers, deep alpine lakes and sub-tropical forest.

Situated on the Pacific's 'Rim of Fire', New Zealand experiences both volcanic and earthquake activity. Rotorua, in the middle of the North Island, is famous for its intense thermal activity in the form of geysers, hot springs and pools of boiling mud.

New Zealand's highest mountain is Mount Cook, in the South Island's Southern Alps. The deep south is famous for its fiords – drowned glacial valleys – while spectacular 'sounds' (large inlets formed from earthquake uplifts) draw visitors to the bottom of the South Island. Over much of this rugged countryside are fertile soils supporting New Zealand's agricultural industry.

Right: a Maori sign of bonding

Government and Economy
New Zealand is a sovereign, independent democratic state and a member of both the United Nations and the Commonwealth. The government is elected every three years. The traditional 'first-past-the-post' electoral system, based on the British parliamentary model, has recently been replaced by a proportional representation system called MMP.

The Government's leader is called the Prime Minister, and the Head of State is the Queen of England, who is represented here by a resident Governor-General.

New Zealand is often thought of as a farming country. Wool, meat and dairy products contribute greatly to its export earnings, though agriculture employs less than 10 percent of the workforce. There are significant natural resources in the country, of which natural gas and coal are particularly abundant.

People and Population
New Zealand has 4 million people, mostly of British descent, with the largest minority (about 12 percent) being Maori of Polynesian origin. The most densely populated area of the country is the northern half of the North Island. About three-quarters of the population are in the North Island, with 25 percent in the Greater Auckland area alone.

New Zealanders are sometimes called Kiwis after the flightless bird that is the country's unofficial national symbol (not after the small furry fruit that also shares the Kiwi name!) You may also hear the term *Pakeha*, which is Maori for Europeans.

MONEY MATTERS

Currency

New Zealand operates a decimal currency system, with one dollar made up of 100 cents. Coins come in denominations of 5¢, 10¢, 20¢, 50¢, NZ$1 and NZ$2. Notes come in NZ$5, NZ$10, NZ$20, NZ$50 and NZ$100 denominations. Check the newspapers for the latest rates of exchange.

Banks and Money Exchange

Trading banks are open between 9.30am and 4.30pm Monday through Friday. Automatic teller machines operate outside these times.

Banking and money exchange facilities are open at New Zealand's international airports to coincide with the arrival and departure of most international flights. More and more Bureau de Change facilities are opening up to serve the main tourist areas.

Credit Cards

Paying by credit card is widely accepted throughout New Zealand.

Travellers Cheques

Travellers cheques can be changed at trading banks, large city hotels and many other trading organisations in the main cities and principal tourist resorts.

Goods and Services Tax

A Goods and Services Tax (GST) of 12.5 percent is applied to the cost of all goods and services in New Zealand, except for purchases at duty-free shops.

Tipping

New Zealanders do not depend on tips for their income and tips are not expected for normal service, even in restaurants, bars and taxis. Tipping for exceptional service, however, is at your discretion. Service charges are not added to hotel or restaurant bills.

GETTING AROUND

Car

With New Zealand host to so much natural beauty, driving offers one of the best ways to see much of the country. The standard of roads is generally high. Multi-lane motorways, however, are limited in their extent – reserved for providing immediate access to and through the major cities. Instead, single-lane State Highways (SH) are the norm.

While motor traffic is generally light by European standards, the winding and narrow nature of some roads means you can only go as fast as the slowest truck. So do not underestimate driving times. Despite an open road speed limit of 100 kph (60 mph), your average driving speed over a long-haul trip is more likely to be around 80 kph (50 mph).

Documents: Drivers and hirers of cars must have a valid licence which can either be a current New Zealand licence, an international licence, or one issued in Australia, Canada, the UK, US, Netherlands, Switzerland, Fiji, South Africa and Germany. Check with your travel agent or New Zealand embassy or consulate before leaving.

Driving Rules: The legal speed limit on open roads in New Zealand is 100 kph (60 mph), while the speed limit in built-up areas is usually 50 kph (30 mph) – but watch for sign-posts. We drive on the left, give way to traffic on the right, and give way to right-turning traffic if we are turning left. The wearing of seat belts is compulsory, as is the wearing of helmets while cycling.

For more detailed information, ask for a booklet on driving in New Zealand from a tourist information office or check with **Land Transport New Zealand** (www.ltsa.govt.nz).

Car Hire: If hiring a car, you would be wise to book in advance. Major international firms such as Avis, Hertz and Budget can have the cars waiting for you at most New

Zealand airports. Independent operators like **Kiwi Car Rentals** (tel: 0800 549 4227; www.carrentals.co.nz) can offer cheaper deals, especially for trips of longer duration.

If you have not pre-booked, tourist information desks at most New Zealand airports can direct you to other operators. Note that the minimum age for renting a car is 21.

Maps: Detailed road maps are available at bookstores and service stations. Reciprocal membership arrangements may be available between the **New Zealand Automobile Association** (www.nzaa.co.nz) in New Zealand and foreign motoring organisations.

Taxis

There are taxis available throughout the country, 24 hours a day. Check the Yellow Pages of the local phone book for a number, or ask at your hotel. Taxis charge an initial flag-down rate, or a call-out fee, in addition to a charge per kilometre travelled. If empty they can be waved down on the street.

Air

New Zealand's two main domestic air carriers are **Air New Zealand** (tel: 0800 737 000; www.airnz.co.nz), and **Qantas** (tel: 0800 808 767; www.qantas.com.au).

Domestic airfares may seem rather expensive (a standard Auckland-Christchurch one-way fare, for example is around NZ$330) but there are plenty of deals around for flying in off-peak times, or for booking ahead from overseas. Security is strict at the airports. Passengers on domestic flights must check in no later than 30 minutes prior to departure. All hand luggage will be screened, and passengers pass through security checks to get to the departure areas. No sharp objects are allowed in carry-on luggage.

Bus

Major cities have extensive local bus services. Check with information offices for details of how they operate.

Coaches also operate **inter-city services** throughout the country. Make sure you reserve seats, especially if travelling during holiday periods. Main operators are **InterCity** (tel: 09 913 6100; www.intercitycoach.co.nz), and **Newmans** (tel: 09 913 6200; www.new manscoach.co.nz).

Train

Passenger services by train have been significantly reduced after a restructuring of the rail network. Only a couple of main routes remain, including a daily service between Auckland to Wellington, and a daily service between Christchurch and Picton.

The **TranzAlpine** (contact Tranz Scenic, tel: 0800 872 46; www.tranzscenic.co.nz) is the most spectacular, taking a route that runs from Christchurch across the Canterbury Plains and through the mountains of the Southern Alps on the way to Greymouth on the West Coast.

Ferry

The North and South Islands are linked by ferries operated by the **InterIslander** and **Lynx** service (tel: 0800 802 802 or 04 498 3302; www.interislandline.co.nz). The ferries sail between Wellington in the North Island and Picton in the South Island (*see page 50*), across the Cook Strait, and carry passengers and vehicles. There are at least three sailings a day, both ways, with the crossing taking about 3 hours on the Interislander service and just over 2 hours on the Lynx.

Transport Passes

If you decide not to drive, one of the best ways to travel is to buy either a **New Zealand Travel Pass** (www.travelpass.co.nz; tel: 03 961 5245) or a **Best of New Zealand Pass** (www.bestpass.co.nz; tel: 04 498 2939). These passes allow a combination of travel on train, bus, ferry and domestic flights at discounted rates.

TRAM TRACKS
CYCLISTS
TAKE CARE

Right: every which way

HOURS AND HOLIDAYS

Business Hours

Business hours are generally Monday to Friday 9am–5pm. Most stores and shops are open Monday to Friday 9am–5.30pm, and Saturday 10am–1pm. Many also stay open late one night a week (till 9pm), usually on Thursday or Friday, and some stores open on Sunday. In tourist areas and resorts, shops are invariably open on Sundays and evenings. Banks are open Monday to Friday 9.30am–4.30pm.

Bars, pubs and taverns open Monday to Saturday from 11am and close between 11pm and 2am depending on their licence. Nightclubs usually open their doors 7.30–8pm and close around 4am.

Public Holidays

1 January: New Year's Day
2 January: Day after New Year's Day
6 February: Waitangi Day
March/April: Good Friday
March/April: Easter Monday
25 April: Anzac Day
First Monday of June: Queen's Birthday
Last Monday of October: Labour Day
25 December: Christmas Day
26 December: Boxing Day

In addition, each province has a holiday to celebrate its anniversary: Northland and Auckland, 29 January; Taranaki, 31 March; Hawke's Bay, 1 November; Wellington, 22 January; Marlborough, 1 November; Westland, 1 December; Canterbury, 16 December; Otago and Southland, 23 March. The holiday is tagged on to the nearest weekend to these dates.

ACCOMMODATION

New Zealand has a wide range of accommodation to suit all budgets. As well as standard hotel and motel accommodation in central locations, other options include 'farm-stays', where you are looked after on a New Zealand farm, or a stay at an exclusive lodge. Both offer unique holiday experiences. For farm-stay details contact **Rural Holidays NZ** (www.ruralhols.co.nz). For luxury lodges contact **Lodges of New Zealand** (www.lodgesofnz.co.nz).

It is advisable to book your accommodation in advance. Apart from contacting the hotel directly or a travel agent, affiliated information centres of **Tourism New Zealand** (www.purenz.com) can help too. Also useful is the guide book published by the **New Zealand Automobile Association** (www.aaguides.co.nz).

An approximate guide to current room rates (standard double inclusive of tax) is:
$\quad$ $ $\quad$ = $\quad$ NZ$90 and below
$\quad$ $$ $\quad$ = $\quad$ NZ$90–180
$\quad$ $$$ $\quad$ = $\quad$ NZ$180–250
$\quad$ $$$$ $\quad$ = $\quad$ NZ$250 and above

Auckland

Heritage Auckland
35 Hobson Street
Tel: 09 379 8553
www.heritagehotels.co.nz
A top class hotel in a mid-city Auckland location near the Sky City casino and walking distance to Viaduct Basin and the Aotea Centre. The building was once an old department store but its glory days are back. Health club and fine-dining restaurant. **$$$$**

Hilton Auckland
147 Quay Street, Princes Wharf
Tel: 09 978 2000
www.hilton.com
One of Auckland's newest five star properties, this boutique hotel occupies prime position at Princes Wharf on Quay Street. Commanding uninterrupted views of the harbour, its 166 rooms and suites are done up in minimalist contemporary style. **$$$$**

SKYCITY Hotel
Corner of Victoria and Federal streets
Tel: 09 363 6000
www.skytower.co.nz
Part of the Sky City complex that includes Sky Tower and Harrah's Casino. Central location with large comfortable rooms, but

Right: luxury lodge-style accommodation

sporting brash décor that typifies casinos. Rooftop pool, bars and restaurants. $$$

New President Hotel
27–35 Victoria Street West
Tel: 09 303 1333
www.newpresidenthotel.co.nz
Comfortable rooms and suites with kitchenettes. Ideally situated between Sky City and Queen Street. $$

Park Towers
3 Scotia Place
Tel: 09 309 2800
www.parktowers-hotel.co.nz
Good value for money. The rooms aren't large but they are tidy and you can get some good views from its location off upper Queen Street. Walking distance to Aotea Square. $$

Parnell's Village Motor Lodge
2 St Stephens Avenue, Parnell
Tel: 09 377 1463
www.parnellmotorlodge.co.nz
Choose between elegant Victorian rooms and modern apartments near Parnell shops. Five minutes from downtown Auckland. $$

Rotorua
Lake Plaza Rotorua Hotel
1000 Eurera Street
Tel: 07 348 1174
www.lakeplazahotel.co.nz
Strategically placed opposite the Polynesian Spa, it has superb views of the lake and thermal areas and is within walking distance of the city centre. $$$

Millennium Rotorua
Corner of Eruera and Hinemaru streets
Tel: 07 347 1234

www.cdlhotels.com
Ask for a room overlooking the Polynesian Pools and Lake Rotorua. You get a great view from the balcony. Friendly staff and good facilities including gym and pool. $$$

Regal Geyserland
424 Fenton Street
Tel: 07 348 2039
www.vacation.co.nz/regal
Million-dollar view over Whakarewarewa Thermal Reserve, and opposite golf course. Helpful management and staff make you feel welcome. $$$

Rydges Rotorua
272 Fenton Street
Tel: 07 349 0099
www.rydges.com/rotorua
Commands panoramic view of Lake Rotorua and Mokoia Island. Within walking distance of the main shopping area. Restaurants, bar and rooftop heated pool. $$$

Princes Gate Hotel
1 Arawa Street
Tel: 07 348 1179
Old colonial-style hotel recapturing bygone era. Near Government Gardens and Polynesian Pools. $$

Wellington
The Duxton
170 Wakefield Street
Tel: 04 473 3900
www.duxton.co.nz
A favourite hotel of business travellers who want to make an impression. Modern facilities with good views from spacious rooms. Good mid-town location near Michael Fowler Centre and the waterfront. Burbury's restaurant on the top floor offers fine silver service dining. $$$$

Inter-Continental Wellington
Corner of Grey and Featherston streets
Tel: 04 472 2722
www.interconti.com
Excellent location by the waterfront, the hotel is a good base for both business and leisure. Has 232 rooms and suites, restaurants, bars and room service, and a good fitness centre with heated pool. $$$$

Above: Auckland's glitzy Sky Hotel

James Cook Hotel Grand Chancellor
147 The Terrace
Tel: 04 499 9500
www.grandhotelsinternational.com
Top management and service in this landmark central hotel; ideal location for shopping. One of the first grand hotels built in Wellington but has kept up with the times. $$$

Victoria Court Motor Inn
201 Victoria Street
Tel: 04 472 4297
www.victoriacourt.co.nz
Located near the city centre the quality units and off-street parking make it a good option for the traveller. From here it is only a short stroll to the eateries of Cuba Street and the shopping of Manners Mall. $$$

Tinakori Lodge Bed and Breakfast
182 Tinakori Street
Tel: 04 939 3478
www.tinakorilodge.co.nz
Close to rail, Botanic Gardens and restaurants in historical Thorndon area. Scrumptious breakfast buffet. $$

Christchurch
Crowne Plaza Hotel
Corner of Kilmore and Durham streets
Tel: 03 365 7799
www.christchurch.crowneplaza.com
Magnificent location on Victoria Square in the central city. Immaculate rooms, spacious corridors and top-class amenities. $$$$

The George Hotel
50 Park Terrace
Tel: 03 379 4560

www.thegeorge.com
A low-rise luxury hotel on a great site across the road from the Avon River and Hagley Park. Nice willow-shaded rooms with balconies. Ten-minute walk to the city centre. Top-rated fine dining restaurant. $$$$

Hotel Grand Chancellor
161 Cashel Street
Tel: 03 379 2999
www.grandc.co.nz
Excellent location in downtown Christchurch and only a short walk from Cathedral Square. Comfortable rooms matched by prompt service. $$$

Latimer Hotel
30 Latimer Square
Tel: 03 379 6760
Low-rise traveller's lodge near city centre with good value rooms and off street parking for your car. $$

Windsor Bed and Breakfast
52 Armagh Street
Tel: 03 366 1503
Bed and breakfast style accommodation in an old Victorian villa. Share facilities; basic, but good. Central location. $$

Queenstown
Novotel Gardens
Corner of Marine Parade and Earl Street
Tel: 03 442 7750
www.novotel.co.nz
Modern hotel on lakefront 200m (219yds) from city centre. Spacious and welcoming foyer gives a hint of the spacious and welcoming nature of the rooms. Management and staff are top class and unobtrusive. $$$$

Nugget Point
Arthur's Point Road
Tel: 03 442 7273
www.nuggetpoint.co.nz
Award-winning boutique property only 10-minutes drive from Queenstown. The suites are impeccably furnished with the more expensive ones featuring stunning views of Shotover River and Coronet Peak. Competent staff magically appear when you need them. Its Birches restaurant is highly recommended. *The* place to go for a real treat. $$$$

Left: Nugget Point's outdoor spa

Copthorne Lakefront Resort

Corner of Adelaide and Frankton roads
Tel: 03 442 8123
www.copthornelakefront.co.nz
Four-star accommodation with 241 cosy rooms, many with views of the lake and mountains. Not in the centre of Queenstown but within walking distance of the main shopping area. Shuttle service available. $$$

Rydges Lakeland Resort

38–54 Lake Esplanade
Tel: 03 442 7600
www.rydges.com/queenstown
Queenstown's largest hotel. Great site by the waterfront. Just a short stroll to Steamer Wharf and into town. Also hosts the award-winning Clancy's Restaurant. $$$

Ambassador Motor Lodge

2 Man Street
Tel: 03 442 8593
Good value for money. Basic facilities but most rooms have lake views. Located at the start of town as you come in from the airport. Nice and friendly staff. $$

HEALTH AND EMERGENCIES

General Health

New Zealand's cities and towns have excellent public water supplies and tap water is always safe to drink.

There are no snakes or dangerous wild animals in New Zealand. Sandflies are prevalent in some areas, but these are effectively countered by insect repellent.

Pharmacies

Pharmacies or chemists are generally open from 9am to 5.30pm weekdays. Some also open on Saturday mornings and for one late night a week. Most major cities also have urgent dispensaries which are open overnight and over the weekends.

Medical and Dental Services

For non-emergencies, full instructions on obtaining assistance are printed in the front of telephone directories. Hotels and motels normally have individual arrangements with

doctors for guests' attention, and they can also assist you in finding a dentist.

New Zealand's medical facilities, both public and private, provide a high standard of treatment. However, services are not free to visitors (except as a result of an accident), so buy adequate medical insurance.

Emergencies

Dial 111 for emergency calls to police, fire or ambulance services.

New Zealand suffers only isolated incidences of serious crime. However, petty crime is a problem. Take precautions to secure and conceal your valuables at all times, and never leave them in a car.

Police

New Zealand police generally do not carry weapons, and you'll find them approachable and helpful.

COMMUNICATIONS AND MEDIA

Post

Post offices generally open Monday to Friday 9am–5pm. In many areas, postal services and stamps are also available from stores or other outlets. Red and white post boxes are found in most main streets.

Telephone

Phone calls made from public telephones to the local area (free call zone) cost 50¢ for unlimited time. There are a mixture of coin-operated machines (that take 10¢ and 20¢ coins) and card-operated machines. Phone cards can be obtained from bookshops.

When calling New Zealand from abroad,

Above: old-fashioned telephone booths

dial 64. When calling within New Zealand, dial 0 before the city code: Auckland (9); Rotorua (7); Wellington (4); Christchurch and Queenstown (3).

To call abroad, first dial the international access code, 00, then the country code.

Mobile phones operate on GSM and 3G networks, provided by **Vodafone** (www.voda phone.com) and **Telecom** (www.telecom.co. nz). You may also consider hiring a mobile phone on arrival in New Zealand, or buying prepaid phone cards, which are available in Vodafone and Telecom shops.

Media

Mass circulation daily newspapers are produced in New Zealand's main centres. *The Herald* in Auckland is the North Island's largest circulation paper, while *The Press* in Christchurch is the South Island's largest. There are also local daily papers published in provincial centres and larger towns. International papers can be found in large bookstores at the main centres.

New Zealand has four national television channels and several local stations. In the main centres, many hotels subscribe to the Sky satellite service for international sports and news links. There are a variety of AM- and FM-band radio stations across the country catering to a wide variety of tastes.

LANGUAGE

New Zealand has two official languages, English and Maori. Nearly everyone speaks English (with a distinctive, often nasal accent). New Zealand has adopted standard English grammar and spelling, but has also added some 'Kiwi-isms' to the vocabulary. You may hear, for instance, the word 'grotty', meaning dirty; or 'chilly bin', a portable cooler used for picnics; or 'grog', for alcohol.

Maori is a language going through a renaissance in New Zealand. It is now being taught in schools and is commonly spoken in some parts of the North Island. The Maori influence is strong in a number of place names, and many words have entered common usage, for example: *Pakeha*, meaning a non-Maori; *kia ora*, for hello; *kai*, for food; and *hangi*, a style of Maori cooking.

OUTDOOR ACTIVITIES

Given New Zealand's diverse and remarkable terrain, it's not surprising that the country is host to a wide variety of outdoor activities. For more information on the following activities, check with tourist information offices in various towns and cities *(see page 99)*. Also try the Tourism New Zealand website at www.purenz.com.

Jet-Boating

Swift flowing and sometimes broad and shallow rivers meant that traditional boats were next to useless in many of New Zealand's waterways. Therefore, a new type of boat was developed here – the jet-boat – using technology that is now common around the world.

There are now numerous operators of river jet-boat rides in New Zealand, the most famous being the **Shotover Jet** operation in **Queenstown** (www.shotoverjet.com; tel: 03 442 8570). A ride on a Shotover Jet takes you at high speeds through the picturesque Shotover River. It remains the premier jet-boating experience, but is followed closely by **Huka Jet** in **Taupo** (www.hukajet.co.nz; tel: 07 374 8572), operating down from the mighty Huka Falls just north of Taupo.

Fishing

New Zealand's waters have proved to be a fertile breeding ground for a wide variety of native and introduced fish species, and the country is regarded as an anglers' paradise. New Zealand also has some of the best dry-fly fishing waters of the world and skilled guides are available in the popular areas.

In the North Island, the **Rotorua/Taupo** area offers rainbow steelhead fishing, requiring at times heavy gear for the deep lakes. Fishing either side of winter (April/May and

Left: the famous Shotover Jet

September/October) is the prime time for catches, with **Lake Taupo** and **Lake Tarawera** being two popular locations.

Summertime (October to April) fly fishing is available countrywide, with the **Tongariro River**, south of Taupo, being one of the best spots in the world.

The South Island offers a wide variety of dry-fly, nymph streamer or lure fishing for brown and rainbow trout from spring through to autumn. East coast rivers such as the **Rakia**, **Waimakariri**, **Rangitata** and **Waitaki** offer superb salmon fishing with the best months being February and March, and the best times very early in the morning.

Fishing licences are available from tackle and sports shops, and a special tourist licence is available for a month of fishing throughout the country.

Big game fishing for marlin also has a fine reputation. The best months are January to May and the **Bay of Islands** is an accessible base, with ample charter boat facilities.

Bungy Jumping

Yes, this is the country where bungy jumping began, with operations in **Queenstown** again leading the way. If you want to throw yourself off a ledge with a rubber band attached to your ankles then there is no shortage of options. One of the latest and highest leaps is the Nevis High-wire, where you jump 134m (440ft) from a platform suspended by wire across the Nevis Gorge. Also popular is the spectacular 71m (233ft) Skipper's Canyon jump-off from a historic bridge spanning the upper reaches of the Shotover River. Equally well known is the site of the first commercial bungy jump in the world – the 43m (141ft) jump off the Kawarau Bridge. For details, contact **A J Hackett Bungy** (tel: 03 442 7100; www.ajhackett.com).

Skydiving

If jumping from a ledge with a rubber band tied to your leg is too passé for you – how about jumping from a plane then? Tandem skydiving has made this thrill accessible to all. Attached to an experienced skydiver by a special harness, there is little you need to do except follow the instructions and keep control of your fear. The bonus with this thrill is the stunning views offered by the plane ride as you circle up above the drop zone. In **Queenstown** have a go with **Skydive Queenstown** (www.nzone.biz; tel: 03 442 5867). At **Fox Glacier** try **Skydive New Zealand** (www.skydivingnz.co.nz; tel: 03 768 4777).

Four-wheel Drive/ATV Adventures

This is a great way to get to some of the more rugged parts of the country. Operators take you through bush, over private beaches, up rivers, usually cooking up a barbecue or providing a picnic along the way. It is bone-shaking fun and you can learn a lot about New Zealand's farming or natural heritage from the drivers. There are good operators in all parts of the country, so check the local tourism offices. In **Queenstown** try **Nomad Safaris** (tel: 03 442 6699; www.nomadsafaris.co.nz).

Rafting

There are many fast flowing rivers in New Zealand and a great way to experience them is in a raft. Rivers range from grade 1 (easy) to grade 5 (extreme) and trips range from a few hours to a few days, depending on the type of adventure you are after. In **Queenstown** try **Challenge Rafting** with trips on the Kawarau River or Shotover River (tel: 03 442 7318; www.raft.co.nz).

Above: leaping off Kawarau Bridge, Queenstown

Whales and Dolphins

More sedate than some of the other adventures mentioned, but a must-do on a trip to New Zealand, is swimming with dolphins or whale watching. The best whale watching is offered in **Kaikoura** by **Whale Watch Kaikoura** (www.whalewatch.co.nz; tel: 03 319 6767). Some of the great mammals you might see are sperm whales, humpback whales and orca. For swimming with dolphins, try **Kings Dolphins Cruises**, based in **Paihia** in the Bay of Islands (tel: 09 402 8288; www.dolphincruises.co.nz).

Skiing/Snowboarding

The rugged New Zealand terrain offers a wide range of skiing in winter – and at much lower prices than in Europe or the US. The two North Island commercial ski fields are **Whakapapa** and **Turoa**, both located on the slopes of the active volcano, Mount Ruapehu (2,796 m/9,177 ft).

With its diverse and spectacular mountainscape, Queenstown is an ideal base for skiing in the Southern Lakes' region. The two largest fields are **Coronet Peak** and **The Remarkables**, both easily reached within the hour from the town. A drive of just over 2 hours from Christchurch can get you to the central South Island slopes of **Mount Hutt** (with one of the longest seasons in the country) or **Porter Heights**.

A fantastic experience – verging on the sublime – is heli-skiing. In this variation of the sport you are whisked by helicopter to slopes of virgin powder amidst mountains of stunning beauty. From Queenstown you can access the **Harris Mountains** or the **Tyndall Glacier**, while from Mount Cook you can ski a stunning run on the magnificent **Tasman Glacier**. Contact **Harris Mountain Heli-skiing** (tel: 03 442 6722; www.heliski.co.nz), or **Heli-ski Queenstown** (tel: 03 442 7733; www.flynz.co.nz).

For general information on skiing in New Zealand visit the following websites: www.nzski.com, www.nzsnowlife.com, www.snow.co.nz.

Parapenting/Hang Gliding

You can do away with the plane ride altogether if you like by trying parapenting. The approach here is to unfurl a canopy that lifts you from the ground as you take off down a hill. Once airborne you gain height and drift lazily around the sky. Again it can be done in tandem with an experienced operator. In **Queenstown**, contact **Flight Park Tandems** (tel: 0800 467 325; www.tandem paragliding.co.nz). In hang gliding, you are strapped to a giant kite (together with the pilot of course!) and literally run off a mountain. In **Queenstown**, **SkyTrek** (tel: 03 442 6311) and **Anti Gravity** (tel: 03 441 8898; www.antigravity.co.nz) are recommended.

USEFUL ADDRESSES

New Zealand has an established network of visitor information centres. The ones in the main cities have a national focus while local information centres provide information about local activities only. All centres can be identified by a distinctive logo featuring a green 'i'. For a full listing of information

Above: a parapenter floats to the ground

offices, check the **Tourism New Zealand** official website at www.purenz.com.

AUCKLAND AND ENVIRONS
New Zealand Visitor Information Centre
137 Quay Street, Princes Wharf
Tel: 09 307 0312
www.aucklandnz.com

Auckland Visitor Information Centre
Atrium, Sky City, Cr Victoria & Federal Streets
Tel: 09 363 7180
www.aucklandnz.com

Bay of Islands Information Centre
Maritime Building, Paihia
Tel: 09 402 7683
www.northland.org.nz

Thames Information Centre
206 Pollen Street, Thames
Tel: 07 868 7284
www.thames-info.co.nz

ROTORUA AND ENVIRONS
Tourism Rotorua
1167 Fenton Street, Rotorua
Tel: 07 348 5179
www.rotoruanz.com

Tauranga Visitor Centre
95 Willow Street, Tauranga
Tel: 07 578 8103
www.nztauranga.com

Mt Maunganui Visitor Centre
Salisbury Avenue, Mt Maunganui
Tel: 07 575 5099
www.nztauranga.com

Taupo Visitor Centre
Tongariro Street, Taupo
Tel: 07 376 0027
www.laketauponz.com

WELLINGTON AND ENVIRONS
Wellington Visitor Information Centre
101 Wakefield St, Wellington
Tel: 04 802 4860
www.wellingtonnz.com

Featherston Visitor Centre
Old Courthouse, SH2

Tel: 04 308 8051
www.wairarapnz.com

Martinborough Visitor Centre
18 Kitchener Street
Tel: 04 306 9043
www.wairarapanz.com

CHRISTCHURCH AND ENVIRONS
Christchurch & Canterbury Visitor Centre
Cathedral Square, Christchurch
Tel: 03 379 9629
www.christchurchnz.net

Picton Visitor Information Centre
The Foreshore, Picton
Tel: 03 573 7477
www.picton.co.nz

Kaikoura Visitor Information Centre
West End, Kaikoura
Tel: 03 319 5641
www.kaikoura.co.nz

Hurunui Visitor Information Centre
49 Amuri Ave, Hanmer Springs
Tel: 03 315 7128
www.hurunui.com

WEST COAST
Franz Josef Glacier Visitor Centre
off SH 6
Tel: 03 752 0796
www.west-coast.co.nz

Fox Josef Glacier Visitor Centre
off SH 6
Tel: 03 751 0807
www.west-coast.co.nz

QUEENSTOWN AND ENVIRONS
Queenstown Travel & Visitor Centre
Corner of Shotover and Camp streets
Tel: 03 442 4100
www.queenstown-vacation.com

Other Useful Websites
www.aaguides.co.nz
www.nz.com
www.tourism.net.nz
www.xtra.co.nz

ACKNOWLEDGEMENTS

Cover	**Fotopress News Picture Agency**
Photography	**Craig Dowling and**
Pages 6C, 76B, 78, 80B, 82, 85, 87, 88, 98	**APA**
13T	**Auckland Institute and Museum**
2/3, 10, 14B, 20, 28, 45, 55, 64, 66, 71T/B, 74, 75	**Marcus Brooke**
86	**Courtesy of Hawke's Bay Tourism**
7T, 56, 61, 68, 70, 96	**Francis Dorai/APA**
72	**Simon Grosset/FSP**
Back cover centre, 59, 84	**Max Lawrence**
93	**Leonardo Media**
13B, 14T, 15, 24B, 25, 37T, 43, 53, 81, 92, 97	**David McGonigal**
83	**New Zealand Tourist Board**
94	**Nugget Point**
47B, 48, 49, 50	**Photosource**
26, 47	**Nick Servian/PhotoNewZealand.com**
23B	**Fotopress News Picture Agency**
5	**Jörg Reuther**
16	**Ralph Talmont/PhotoNewZealand.com**
Back cover top, 7B, 11, 29, 42, 65T/B, 67	**Luca Tettoni Photography**
12	**Terence Barrow Collection**
8/9	**VPA Images**
24T	**Robert Wallace**
6B, 27T/B, 51T, 58T, 63	**Angela Wong/APA**

Cartography	**Maria Donnelly**
Cover Design	**Klaus Geister**
Production	**Caroline Low**

© APA Publications GmbH & Co. Verlag KG Singapore Branch, Singapore

credits

INDEX